YOUR BALANCED AND BOLD LIFE

Copyright @ 2024 by Stacey Olson

Published by AIMPATH Publishing

PO Box 37092
Regina, Saskatchewan, Canada
S4S 7K3

All rights reserved. No part of this book may be reproduced or transmitted in any form or by any means, electronic or mechanical, including photocopying and recording, or for informational or retrieval systems without the written permission of the author, except for "fair use" of brief quotes in articles, reviews, and social media.

The author of this book does not dispense medical advice or prescribe the use of any technique as a form of treatment for physical, mental, or emotional issues, either directly or indirectly. This book is not a substitute for counselling, mental health care, or any form of diagnosis, therapy, or treatment. The intent of the author is only to offer information of a general nature to help you in your quest to create balance in your life. The reader is fully responsible for their physical, mental, and emotional health, including all choices, decisions and results. In the event that you use information in this book for yourself or recommend it to others, the author and publisher assume no responsibility for your actions.

Cover design: Vanessa Mendozzi
Cover and author bio photos: Carla van Heerden
Editor: Rachel Small

Paperback ISBN: 978-1-7383823-2-3
e-book ISBN: 978-1-7383823-1-6
Hardcover ISBN: 978-1-7383823-3-0

1st edition, June 2024

YOUR BALANCED AND BOLD LIFE

WORK LESS, LIVE MORE,
AND BE YOUR BEST

STACEY OLSON

*Dedicated to my husband, Kenton,
and kids, Brittany, Carter, and Emmett—
because the rest of it doesn't matter without you.*

A NOTE TO YOU, THE READER.

To the one who wants to feel happier, be more present, and have the time and energy to be there for your family, excel in your career, and take care of yourself, too.

The one who also feels this might be impossible with such a busy life and in a world that expects more and more of you, when you have little more to give.

I get it.

I once thought that balance in my life was unlikely. I deep down wanted it, and there was a part of me that believed there had to be a way, but I didn't know how to make it happen.

I now know that there is a path to being happier, balanced, and successful—for me and for you.

Yes, YOU.

You can work less, live more, and be your best, both in your work and personal life. Even with the constant demands and messy everyday life.

In fact, it's in those small, everyday messy moments that positive change happens. The icing on the cake is that when you create more balance in your life, you'll perform even better and lead even stronger.

You're reading this book for a reason.

Be bold. Decide today that you'll no longer settle for the way things are. Because your life is happening now.

So, let's not waste another moment and get started!

If someone you know comes to mind as you read these pages and you feel they could also benefit from the perspectives and tools shared, please recommend this book to them. Together, let's create a positive ripple effect, with more balance and presence in how we live and lead.

CONTENTS

Foreword. Meghan's Experience   xi

Introduction. Your Life Is Happening Now   1

PART 1. TAKE BACK CONTROL OF YOUR DAYS AND FOCUS ON WHAT REALLY MATTERS

Chapter 1. Be Real with Yourself – What Badge Do You Wear?   23

Chapter 2. Own Your Time, Your Mindset, and What's Possible   41

Chapter 3. Live and Lead with Your Values   61

Chapter 4. Protect Your Time and Energy with Boundaries   77

Chapter 5. Get Clear on Your Real Priorities and What Matters Less   99

Chapter 6. Say 'No' So You Can Say 'Yes' to What Matters More   119

PART 2. CALM YOUR BUSY MIND, BE PRESENT, AND ENJOY YOUR DAYS MORE

Chapter 7. Be Present, Not Perfect   143

Chapter 8. Step Out of the Overwhelm   165

Chapter 9. Turn Down the Volume on Worry and Guilt   183

Chapter 10. Feel Confident in Yourself and Your Choices   199

Chapter 11. Experience More Joy and Less Stress   219

PART 3. BE YOUR BEST FOR YOURSELF AND OTHERS (EVEN WITH MESSY LIFE)

Chapter 12. Navigate Tougher Times with More Ease and Resilience	241
Chapter 13. Make Yourself a Priority AND Be There for Others	257
Chapter 14. Living YOUR Balanced and Bold Life	271
A Final Nudge. Be the Positive Ripple	285
Acknowledgments	289
References	291
About The Author	295

Foreword

MEGHAN'S EXPERIENCE

*Sometimes our moments of struggle offer
our biggest opportunities for growth.*

During a particularly difficult week in the past year, I was navigating work demands and taking care of our children when my husband suddenly needed emergency surgery, and I became sick—all at the same time!

I felt a tremendous amount of guilt over falling behind at work, not being able to care for my husband because I was sick myself, and having very little energy to be emotionally available, patient, or fun for our young children.

Deep down, I felt that I was failing on all fronts.

That's when Stacey's words flipped the script for me.

She invited me to reflect on what I had accomplished that week and how I continued to show up for my family and my job, despite everything that had happened. This helped me realize that I had been prioritizing what mattered most, letting go of the rest, and to stop being so hard on myself.

That day served as a huge 'aha' moment for me. My expectations of myself were completely unrealistic, and I would never hold a friend or colleague to the expectations or pressure I had put on myself.

In the past, I often found myself thinking about what impact I want to make in my life and how I want to be remembered. I have always known that being a kind, loving, compassionate person and having strong relationships with the people I love are most important to me.

However, what I hadn't appreciated was that, despite holding these core values, I often made decisions that were in opposition with them. I would choose to work at night instead of talking with my husband. I would choose to clean the kitchen instead of engaging with my children. I would neglect to exercise regularly (because who has time for that!) despite knowing the difference it made in my ability to show up and feel my best. My Outlook calendar at work dictated most of my schedule and days!

I used to believe that I didn't have a choice.

What I learned as I went through the journey working with Stacey—and what you'll learn from this book—is that I thought that I didn't have enough time for everything, but the truth was I couldn't afford NOT to ensure I was living the life I wanted and spending my time in a way that is aligned with what's most important to me.

Now, **I believe that I have a choice** about how to spend my time and show up in my life. To get to this place, I had to get real with myself about the fact that no one else was going to swoop in and change things for me. If I wanted to change my life, my relationship with work, and my stress level, I had to take ownership over that and do it myself.

Thankfully, while the initiative to make a change was mine, I wasn't alone in this journey.

Stacey is open and real about the challenges we all face, and she offers a path to creating more balance and success in our lives, while being kinder to ourselves along the way. In *Your Balanced and Bold Life,* she shares the same powerful ideas and tools she offered me—along with very relatable personal anecdotes—to support you on your journey to balance and success, however you define them for yourself.

I still think of the 'aha' I had that week when I was struggling with the simultaneous demands of work, caring for my family, and being sick myself. I truly think that going through that experience—and now having the lesson to draw on in difficult moments—helps me work through challenges better. I can remain balanced, appreciate myself and all that I do, and be the person I want to be. I can *be present, not perfect.*

This book will help you experience this, too, and get back in touch with what truly matters to you.

Enjoy!

Meghan Devitt
The Balanced Leader™ former client

Introduction

YOUR LIFE IS HAPPENING NOW

"What you do every day matters more than what you do once in a while."

– GRETCHEN RUBIN

In 2015, my corporate career came to an end. Even though I worked at a great company and had a bright future in the project portfolio management world, I'd made the bold decision to leave.

My intuition said it was time to make a change.

My going-away party took place in a small room at a restaurant, and all my favourite people from work showed up (if you're ever wondering how you're really doing, quit your job and you might just hear the nicest things). One VP, who always seemed to have a grounded perspective on work and life, asked me, "What's the real reason you're going, Stacey?"

I'd told everybody I wanted more flexibility and fulfillment, and that was true. But there was more to it (so much more, which I'll share throughout this book). I thought about it for a moment and then told him the deeper reason: "I don't want to wait for something really bad or tragic to happen for me to wake me up to the fact that I'm missing my life."

That VP told me that I'd figured out much earlier in life what most people figure out when they are fifty or sixty—that life is meant to be more living and less stressing or grinding it out. *Okay, phew*, I thought. (I was only thirty-six then!)

This wasn't the first time in my life, though, that I'd heard that whisper in my head.

You're missing your life.

This went through my mind several years earlier, when I first desired a better work-life balance. I really, *really* cared about doing great work and performing at a high level. I had a strong work ethic (which I had to redefine for myself years later) and prided myself on going above and beyond. I was also feeling way too busy and spread thin. I'd just come back to work after my first maternity leave and was figuring out how to juggle my work with a toddler in the mix. One particular day, I remember sitting in a team meeting for a planning session on employee engagement results. Lack of resources and work-life balance were the top two issues. This wasn't anything new, and the resourcing issue always seemed to trump and take the focus. I remember wondering, *Why isn't anyone paying attention to the whole work-life balance thing?* It's when I first had this nudge, this feeling that there had to be a better way to approach our work and how we live our lives. But we just stayed in the same old grind—and seriously out of balance.

You're missing your life.

About a year before I left my corporate career, that same voice whispered in my head. It was around the time when I made the bold decision to stop overworking, set a strong boundary between my work and personal time, and get back to a forty-hour workweek DURING the most demanding time of my corporate career. I'd been working most evenings and weekends—sixty- to eighty-hour weeks—and felt like I was drowning in everything I "had" to do. I was exhausted and overwhelmed every single day. I still showed up pretty well at work (or so I thought) but had very little energy or patience left by the time I got home. My work got the best side of me, and my husband and kids got the worst side.

In my defense (and yours, too, if this is you), I had very little left in the tank to give.

You're missing your life.

The voice whispered in my head again when I was on summer vacation at the lake a few weeks before I gave my notice at work. I was spending time with my kids in the backyard at our cabin but my mind was elsewhere. My thoughts were racing about everything going on back at work. *What did I forget? Is everything taken care of? Does my team have what they need? I'm so mad that I was asked to skip my vacation. Are people upset with me for not being at work right now? I forgot to send that email!* While my mind was distracted, my kids were playing right in front of me. I was physically there with my family, but not present with them or the current experience AT ALL.

This feeling of missing out on my life was at the heart of why I was leaving my corporate career. While it was true that I wanted more flexibility and fulfillment, what I deep down wanted was to be more present and enjoy my life. To turn off my racing mind. To stop worrying and stressing out about work and what everyone else would think of me if I didn't keep up. To not have a day where I regretted that I hadn't slowed down the pace and had more time and presence for what really mattered to me.

By the time I quit, I'd already figured out how to be more in control of my workload, keep strong boundaries between my work and personal time, prioritize better, and say no. But I hadn't yet figured out how to calm my busy mind and be *mentally* present. I felt as though I was walking a fine line between high performance and being weighed down by all the pressure (most of which I was putting on myself) as if everything could all come crashing down at any moment. I had a better work-life balance in the traditional sense—as in, I was working fewer hours—but I still felt as if I were going through the motions each day.

Looking back, I now understand that I didn't have to leave my corporate career to be present and enjoy my life—to *feel* balanced. Learning how to be present, find joy each day, and practice mindfulness has changed the game for me. We waste so much time and mental energy in worry, overwhelm, and overthinking our every move. You have no idea (or at least I didn't)!

To create more balance in your life, it will take a big shift in how you're *showing up in your life*. This doesn't come from doing something once in a while or from one huge, sweeping change. It comes from being intentional about how you think and show up day-to-day. In the small, everyday moments—that's where you can be more present, self-aware, and make new choices. Choices that are more aligned with what success in your life looks like for you and the person, leader, or parent you want to be.

Are you feeling like you may be missing out on your life? Is that voice whispering to you, too? If so, you're in the right place. Whatever your reason for picking up this book, this is the perfect time to have done so. I believe you're meant to be reading it now and that you're more than capable and ready to create your own balanced and bold life, starting today.

I'm excited and grateful to be on this journey with you and to help you work less, live more, and be your best self—yes, even with the constant demands and messiness of everyday life—so that you can have more time and presence for what really matters to YOU.

YOUR BIG SHIFT

I don't want it to take years for you to get to where I got to. I don't want you to wake up and pay attention only because something really bad happened to you or you're utterly burned out. I don't want you to wait until you're fifty or sixty to really enjoy your life (but better late than never!). When I was thirty, I'd say to myself, "I can't wait to really enjoy my life when I retire." This sounds absurd to me now. Retirement was a LONG way away back then!

I want to inspire you to think about and do something different. Now. Not in five years, or one year, or six months, but right now. No matter your age or your circumstances or your position. No matter how burned out or busy you may be.

Maybe you're working too many hours and want to get back to a regular workweek. Maybe you want to work even fewer hours, perhaps a four-day workweek, so you can spend more time with your kids or have more time for yourself. Maybe you want to feel more on top of things at work and not so overwhelmed every day. Maybe you want to get back to enjoying your days and feel better. Or maybe you want to quit your demanding job and find something more peaceful—and less demanding.

Before you go down the "quit" path, I want you to consider something.

Quitting won't necessarily solve things

We tend to take ourselves where we go. So, there's a good chance you'll take your unhelpful habits and tendencies somewhere else if you don't shift how you think and operate at a foundational level. Especially if you're a driven and ambitious person.

Now, quitting might be the right choice for you (I don't regret my decision to leave my corporate career). But maybe, *just maybe*, you'd be better off learning how to create more balance and be more effective where you're at now. To give yourself permission to align your actions with your values. To ask for what you need and want. To protect your personal time and prioritize better. To say 'no' way more. To let go of feeling so guilty and worrying about what other people will think. To feel more confident in yourself and your choices. To lead by example for others who are too busy and burning out, too. To let your desire to quit give you the inner motivation to do something different now (because if you don't change your ways, you know where this will end).

Looking back, I'm so thankful that I didn't quit my corporate career when I first decided I wanted to stop working so much and to create more balance in my life. It forced me to learn how to keep boundaries, prioritize better during the workday, and say no in a way that kept my relationships strong, even while I was so nervous at first doing it. Had I not learned the messy lessons I'll share with you in this book, I'm certain I would have carried my tendency to overwork into my business and become a burned-out business owner—and *still* be missing out on my life.

By the end of this book, you'll know how to get back in the driver's seat and make your own big shift. You'll learn how to take back control of your days and focus on what really matters, calm your busy mind and enjoy your days more, and be there for others while making yourself a priority too—in practical, encouraging, and empowering ways.

I genuinely believe in you. You CAN do this! Wherever you're at and whatever your reason for picking up this book, you can make changes now, in your current situation, that will transform your life.

THIS BOOK IS FOR YOU

You likely work hard, you're driven and, while you might be proud of what you're achieving so far, you're also feeling that you may be on a path of burnout or want more space for what's important at work, for your family, and for yourself. You're tired of always having to be "on." You wish that you didn't constantly worry about not meeting others' expectations or feel guilty about not doing enough. You're overwhelmed and pulled in too many directions between work and home, and want to feel a greater sense of accomplishment instead of always behind.

You want to get back to having a sense of control in your days. You want to slow down the pace and enjoy your personal time, but you're not sure how to do this while still performing at a high level and being successful in your career. Deep down, you simply want to feel good. To be more present and patient with your loved ones. To make yourself a priority and not feel selfish. To take care of your physical and mental health. To be a confident leader for your team. To be happier, balanced, and successful. To not miss out on your life.

Whatever it is that's most important to you and your reason for being here.

> **Thankfully, there is a path forward! You don't have to settle for the way things are or feel resigned to your current circumstances.**

Many people are waking up to the fact that their well-being is essential. They're done with feeling exhausted and overwhelmed each day. They want to stop working so much or constantly thinking about work. They're no longer willing to compromise their values, mental health, or relationships to be "successful." They want to be more present, enjoy life, and lead with their own version of success.

In essence, this book is for anyone feeling overwhelmed or burned out, caught between the demands of their work and personal lives, and wanting more balance in life and within themselves. It's for leaders who aspire to set a healthier balance for their teams and families. And for those of you who have come to a point of reevaluation and feel as if you're missing out on your life, too.

Keep in mind that I am a woman and a mom, and many of my clients are as well, so this book does have that extra lens to reflect the experiences of women and working parents juggling career and family responsibilities and seeking to balance these roles effectively. That said, the lessons and tools are universal.

Trust that you're here for a reason and can take something valuable away from this book regardless of your role or circumstance or gender or reason for making a change. You're not alone in the way you feel and what you experience.

There's a more fulfilling and enjoyable path to being successful, and it looks different from the one we've been traditionally taught to follow—the one where you have to work harder or sacrifice your personal time or your health to be successful, or sacrifice your career to slow things down. This isn't necessary. Instead, let's sacrifice the overwhelm and the worry and the overworking. You really can "have it all". Whatever having it all looks like for you.

BUT this means giving yourself permission to stop trying to *do* it all.

WHAT IT REALLY TAKES TO "HAVE IT ALL"

Let's imagine for a moment that you really could have it all—that what you desire deep down for your work and your personal life is possible for you. Can you see it? Can you feel it? Not what you think you should do or what others expect of you or what you see others—who are stuck being busy, busy, busy—doing.

What does balance look and feel like for YOU?

What does it feel like when you no longer sacrifice your personal time or being present with your family to keep up with your workload? When you don't believe that you need to sacrifice doing great work to enjoy your life or to take care of your well-being? When you're no longer rushing from one thing to the next and instead living life at a pace that's right for you?

Have you thought about who you want to be—as a leader, as a parent, as a person? How you want to live and show up in your life? What success looks like for you? What if you were to give yourself permission to go for that vision?

Close your eyes, take a deep breath, and see and feel it. Right now.

You may assume that you can't have it all. But you can—when you get clear on what really matters to you and are intentional about creating that kind of life.

Your own version of having it all.

Once you know what you're aiming for, you can take steps toward creating that life. And you'll have the courage to let go of the rest in time. Is it easy? No. But it IS easier than being overwhelmed, burned out, and feeling as if you're barely keeping up every single day. Is it perfect? Definitely not, but nothing in life is perfect. *Be present, not perfect*—this is my mantra these days. Is it possible for you? One-hundred-percent yes. But you need to be willing to go for it and open yourself up to what's possible and to a different way of thinking about and approaching your days (don't worry—I'll help you!).

As you move toward your own version of having it all, you must also **be kind to yourself and grant yourself grace.** You've been doing your best and there's nothing wrong with you. You must also understand that doing your best doesn't necessarily mean *being* your best. But don't worry, your best is there. All the stress and overwhelm is just hiding it! One of my favourite Maya Angelou quotes is "Do the best you can until you know better. Then when you know better, do better." This book will help you know better. You can then be and do better—without being so darn hard on yourself.

WHAT DOES BALANCE EVEN LOOK LIKE?

Before we go any further, let me be clear about what I mean by *balance* (because the word has a lot of baggage attached to it). Balance is about creating more harmony in your life—and within yourself. It's about having the time and presence for ALL the important areas of your life. It's about making your happiness and well-being a priority and feeling more peaceful and centered even when life around you seems chaotic.

Work-life balance is a funny phrase when you think about it, as it implies that there's work and then there's life. But work IS a part of your life. As are your family, friends, health, personal interests, and more. These areas are all important, and they all intersect. Often though, work consumes more time, at the expense of those other important areas. The thing is, when you operate from a place of overwhelm and exhaustion, or sacrifice what matters to you to be "successful," your performance suffers, your relationships suffer, and everything is harder than it needs to be.

So how can you possibly create more balance when there are so many demands and expectations coming at you?

People discount balance, saying it's a myth or impossible, because they equate it to perfection or equal hours. Or because they haven't yet figured out that there's a different path to success. Or because, frankly, balance isn't important to them (they're probably not reading this book!). But when we believe that balance is unattainable, we aren't aspiring to something better. We're resigning ourselves to "this is just the way things are." And we end up overcommitted, stressed out and our days out of control.

Let's go back to one of those arguments. Many people believe that balance means equal hours spent on different aspects of life. But this math just doesn't compute. The concept of dividing hours equally assumes that everyone has the same values, needs, and priorities, which isn't the case. Different people thrive in different conditions—some require more personal downtime to recharge while others find more energy and fulfillment in their professional accomplishments. Our lives are also dynamic. Our needs and priorities change over time or in different stages of our lives (or sometimes week-to-week), so we must be open to shifting our boundaries, priorities and even values as the seasons of our life change.

When you're more balanced, you're better able to focus on the right things at the right times. You know what really matters in both your work and personal life, and you make choices that align with these things (rather than trying to do it all). You're also able to disconnect from work and be more present where you are. You might keep great boundaries, but if you're still thinking or stressing out about work when you're with your family or on vacation, you're not going to feel very balanced. This comes with making yourself a priority and honouring what you need to be and feel your best. When we feel good, we enjoy our days more, lead stronger, perform better, and show up with people more fully.

Balance *will* look different for different people. It's not a one-size-fits-all approach or equal hours or the idea that one day everything will be perfect.

You don't find balance. You create it.

You create it based on your own version of having it all and what works for you.

There will be ups and downs—that's life. Unexpected things will happen and the demands will keep on coming. This is the messiness of life that we all face. But we can take more ownership of our days (and life) and learn how to navigate the challenges and demands with more focus, calm, and ease.

Creating balance in your life comes with a daily intention in who you're being and making choices right for you, especially in those small, everyday moments.

WHAT ABOUT BEING BOLD?

Being bold means being willing to take risks, trust in yourself more, and not just do what everyone else is doing. It's being courageous when you face uncertainty and make choices that might challenge norms. I'll tell you this up front: to make your own big shift and create balance in your life, it's going to take a different way of thinking and approaching your days—even though others around you might be doing things in their own way. But it's so incredibly worth it.

Now, you might be thinking: I see people move up in their careers *because* they put in the long hours and hustle. Yes, you could do it that way. But is that what success *really* looks like for you? I work with many executives and senior leaders who appear to be successful because of the hustle, but they too are wanting to learn how to slow down the pace, take care of themselves, and be more focused on the things that matter instead of spread so thin. And, quite frankly, there's a shift in the world and the workforce toward working less and taking better care of our well-being, so you might as well figure it out now. What if you could be the positive example for others?

When you're taking steps to live your balanced and bold life, you get to the heart of what you really want and what really matters both in your work and personal life. You make choices with intention. You find a pace that's right for you. You enjoy your days and your life so much more. It doesn't matter so much to you if others do it a different way.

Besides, it's no longer sustainable to keep operating the way you are (you know this deep down), and it's well-proven that high performance, happiness, and balance go together.

BALANCE IS A STRATEGIC MOVE

Creating more balance in your life isn't just important when it comes to feeling happier, being more present, and having time for what really matters to you. It's also a strategic move that we need in a world with so many demands and expectations.

We can't keep saying yes to everyone!

Many people are no longer willing to work so much or hurt their mental health and well-being to get the job done. They're no longer willing to sacrifice themselves or burn themselves out. Again, the workforce is changing and, if you lead a team, you're less likely to find people who will grind it out day after day. People want more flexibility and a better work life.

Consider these numbers. Recent research shows that "while 80 percent of executives say well-being is a top priority, nearly 90 percent of workers think their work life is actually getting worse. And 57 percent of employees are considering quitting their job for one that better supports their well-being." This is something to pay attention to! The good news is that people are far more open to a new way of working. They're ready for a shift.

The compromise has gone too far

Step back and look at the bigger picture for a moment. If your work life is getting worse—or not any better—it's time for you to pay attention. Remember, your life is happening now. Not when you retire, when your kids get older, when you get that promotion or that project done, or when your company changes. Right now.

While organizations and leaders must take the well-being of their people more seriously and look at what they can do to create a better work environment, you as an individual must take one-hundred-percent responsibility for your life. If you wait for your company or someone else to change, you might be waiting a long time. You lead by example.

Even though balance and happiness are correlated with high performance (we'll go deeper into this in Chapter 2), they're missing in a lot of organizations, often because people are overloaded doing a lot of things that don't truly move the needle. I'm sure you can think of a meeting or task or project that's a complete waste of time. You might be waiting for those above you or external circumstances to change instead of driving it for yourself and your team.

How do I know this? Because this was me for many years! The unexpected thing that happened when I started to take back control of my days and balance my life was that I performed even better and became a stronger leader. This journey completely transformed my relationship with my work, with my husband and kids, and, most importantly, with myself. This journey has changed my clients' lives. It's the journey I'm inviting you on with this book.

Small changes can make a big difference

Think of a rock being dropped in water—it creates ripples in every direction. Similarly, a lack of balance and too much stress creates negative ripples in every direction. It impacts your connection with your loved ones. Your leadership and performance. Your peace and happiness. A good night's sleep!

When you start to make some of the positive changes we explore in this book, you'll start to see positive ripples in every direction as well. When you are intentional and make small daily changes to be more balanced, you'll:

- Have more time and energy for what really matters
- Be more present and connected with your loved ones
- Have stronger relationships with others
- See improved performance at work and in other areas of your life
- Lead stronger and feel more confident in your choices
- Feel happier and more peaceful (and sleep better!)
- Show up as a better version of yourself at work and at home
- Be the positive ripple for others.

These are just a few of the reasons why creating balance is a strategic move. *What's your reason?*

OUR JOURNEY

I wrote this book for you. I also wrote it for me. It's the book I wish I'd had all those years ago when I was burning out and that voice was whispering that I was missing out on my life. *And* it's the book that I still need today to help me remain balanced as I grow my business, keep my relationships strong, and navigate the overwhelm, doubts, and worries that still pop up.

I share personal stories and messy lessons, empowering perspective shifts, and practical strategies and tools in a way that is designed to help you figure out what will work for YOU. What you'll discover in these pages isn't just the result of my own journey and training but also from years spent coaching hundreds of clients who made bold changes in their own lives—their struggles, questions, insights, and actions are subtly woven throughout the pages and shaped the guidance offered in the book and the work that I do.

It's structured into three transformative parts, each designed to guide you through a different aspect of creating balance in your life.

Part 1: Take back control of your days and focus on what really matters. This part is about stepping back and seeing the bigger picture, expanding your self-awareness, and getting clear on what balance looks like for you and the mindset you'll need to create it. You'll learn how to live and lead with your values, keep stronger boundaries to protect your time and energy, and get clear on your real priorities (and what matters less). You'll learn how to say no with more confidence and ease so that you can say yes to what matters more and stop overcommitting yourself. You'll be better able to balance your workload, family, personal responsibilities, and "me time." And you'll feel more empowered to let go of doing it all.

Part 2: Calm your busy mind, be present, and enjoy your days more. This part is all about learning how to build mindfulness and be present (not perfect), step out of the overwhelm, and turn down the volume on worry and guilt. You'll learn how to feel more confident in yourself, so you can make choices that are aligned with your values and needs rather than let fear—or other people—decide for you. You'll explore how to experience more joy and less stress in your life so you can feel good and enjoy your days more. You'll feel more balanced when you learn how to take care of your mind, be present, and *feel better*. You'll also free up so much time and mental energy and be able to take action more easily on what you uncovered in Part 1—it will be easier to say no when you let go of the guilt!

Part 3: Be your best for yourself and others (even with messy life). By this part, you'll truly understand that it's hard to be your best when you're exhausted and pulled in too many directions. You'll learn how to better navigate the tougher days with more calm, ease, and resilience, even when life throws you a bigger curveball. You'll learn how to better balance making yourself a priority and being there for others, so you can be more patient and connected in your relationships—and have a positive influence. You'll understand what it really takes to live your balanced and bold life, grant yourself grace knowing that your best will look different on different days, and better listen to what you need on those days when you have less to give. You'll lead by example and be a positive ripple for yourself and others.

Your personal journey

By the end of the book, you'll have made your own big shift in how you're showing up in your life, and it will be in a way that is aligned with what balance looks like for you. This is not "one and done," though. Change is a work in progress—we use our best to make us better and continually refine our values, boundaries, and priorities so that they serve us. You can come back to your insights and this book time and time again.

While we all have different experiences, I hope that you can relate to my stories and know that you're not alone or selfish for wanting a healthier and more enjoyable pace. I offer you perspectives, practical actions and tools, and simple, powerful questions to prompt greater self-awareness and action that you can put into practice to create more balance in a way that *fits your life*. Each chapter ends with a **be bold** action. These are meant to encourage you to take small, immediate action, as this is what will help you create meaningful change day after day.

While some of the information presented might seem basic and perhaps familiar, we're often expected to understand many of the concepts in this book without being shown *how* to do it or tailor them to our own lives. My intention is to bridge that gap. It's also important to note that while this book presents the journey as a chapter-by-chapter process, change like this isn't a linear experience. You can make gains in one area and see the positive "ripple" impact in others.

Make your way through the book, take action as you go, and weave into your life what's most helpful for you right now. Pay attention to what stands out to you (it stands out for a reason) and feel free to ignore what doesn't resonate with you right now. Go through one chapter at a time or read the entire book at once so you get the full picture before returning to the Self-Awareness and Action questions at the end of each chapter. I suggest using a journal to capture your answers to the questions, or you can download the accompanying workbook. Trust your intuition and do what's right for you.

My intention is to show you a new path forward, to inspire you to create your own big shift in how you show up in your life, and to help you see more choices and possibilities, starting today.

This is the permission you've been waiting for to create your own balanced—and bold—life.

For the supporting workbook and other book resources, go to **www.staceyolson.ca/balance**.

YOU HAVE A CHOICE

The most empowering perspective and belief to hold is: *I have a choice*. While much is happening outside of your control, what's within your control are your thoughts, beliefs, and actions. You can choose to take ownership of your days and your life, and you have a choice in every moment. I'll help you see more choices available to you.

Real change starts with you.

You can continue to "succeed" like everyone else or you can decide to find a different way to be successful—a way that offers more balance, happiness and presence. You can wait for something really bad to happen or to have your "enough is enough" moment. Or you can simply decide TODAY that enough is enough and it's time for change.

You have a choice from here. It's time to stop settling for the way things are. Because your life is happening NOW. In this very moment. And you might miss it if you don't slow down and pay attention!

Of course, when you're overloaded and overwhelmed, knowing where to start to take back control of your days can be hard to figure out. In the first part of this book, I'll share more about what led to my own "enough is enough" moment and we'll explore how you too can turn things around. Let's begin with some self-awareness.

PART 1

Take Back Control of Your Days and Focus on What Really Matters

Chapter 1

BE REAL WITH YOURSELF – WHAT BADGE DO YOU WEAR?

"Almost everything will work again if you unplug it for a few minutes, including you."

– Anne Lamott

When my kids were younger, they went to a daycare in our neighborhood's elementary school. Most days when my husband and I picked the kids up, a young woman named Valerie would be working. She often told me that she thought my husband and I were the "perfect power couple" (I'm not kidding). We'd be in our suits, smiling, strolling in together after work each day and, to her, we were the shining example of what it was like to have a successful career and a family.

Usually when Valerie said this, I'd smile and rush on by (because I was probably late picking up the kids). One day, though, I stopped to chat and give her a sense of "real life."

"Valerie," I said, "Here's what my life is really like. Today was nonstop at work. I was in meetings all day long and I haven't eaten lunch. I'm exhausted and I have a disaster of a house to clean, no supper plan, and a few hours of work to do tonight once the kids are in bed. I've been here for five minutes, the kids are already driving me crazy, and I yelled at them for taking too long (again). Each day feels like a blur between work and home. Yes, I have a great job and family, and I know I have a good life. But I also feel like I'm just barely getting by and I'm constantly worried about what other people will think if I can't keep up with it all. Most of the time, I feel guilty that I'm letting someone down. I'm more impatient and fighting with my husband and kids than I'd like to admit. And to top it off, I have one or two panic attacks a week trying to get the kids out the door in the morning and myself to work on time for 8:00 a.m. meetings. This is what most days and weeks are like. So, I wouldn't quite say this is a success or that we're the perfect power couple."

Valerie simply shrugged and said "Okay" with a smile before going about her day. I imagine she hadn't really cared to learn about the inner workings of my life!

I worked at a great company, was recognized as a high performer, and had a bright future in my career. I was married to my favourite person and had three awesome kids. I also worked most evenings and weekends and was overwhelmed every single day. Sometimes I'd even secretly wish I'd get seriously sick because then I'd have a "good enough reason" to slow down the pace. (Ever think that? No, it's just me?) That I'd wish for anything but my health sounds like absolute nonsense to me now.

My "enough is enough" moment was still a few months away, but the day I gave my heartfelt speech to Valerie was the start of my journey to create balance in my life, which I'll unravel over the next few chapters. There was a perfect storm of change brewing. Although I took back control of my days relatively quickly once I decided to make a change, it was a *very* long time coming.

THE MESSY LESSON AND KEY SHIFT

While my life looked great on the outside, and it seemed as if I had it all together, things looked very different up close. I was a scattered mess on the inside. In fact, I was burning out and didn't even realize it. Most people in my life had no idea I was struggling so much. I wasn't necessarily trying to hide anything—I was just sucking it up and going through the motions each day, thinking that this was what life was like with a young family, a career, and everything else. I was operating in a state of constant busyness and stress.

This is a VERY familiar reality for many people. Maybe even you.

Any meaningful change starts with becoming more self-aware and willing to be honest with yourself about how you're *really* doing—without judgment.

This isn't about being hard on yourself. It's about being real with yourself.

As hard as that time was, I'm grateful because it led to a big shift in how I show up in my life. Only once I started to slow down for a moment and acknowledge how much I was struggling and that the pace wasn't sustainable did I begin to make some significant, yet simple, changes to balance my life—and myself.

Our biggest growth can come from our biggest struggles. So how about we agree right now that instead of being harder on yourself for what you're not doing or what's not going well, you'll use this book to empower yourself to make your own big shift and step out of the busyness. Deal?

THE BADGE OF BUSYNESS

You likely have a lot on your plate. Things are busy at work. And at home. You push yourself, have high standards, and feel as though you have something to prove. Somehow, you're juggling all the balls (but silently worrying you'll drop one ... or more). You might feel as if success equals how many hours you're putting in, or how many activities you have your kids in, or simply how busy you are. Anytime someone asks you how you're doing (or you ask someone else), the words "I'm busy" come out of your mouth. I get it.

The badge of busyness is subtle yet pervasive. This badge isn't tangible; you won't find it pinned to a shirt, but its presence is unmistakably felt. It symbolizes a set of societal expectations in a world where our worth and success are measured by how busy our schedules are. A world where being constantly engaged in work, family responsibilities, and social commitments isn't just the norm—it's glorified.

For women, this badge can take on additional layers. It's not just about being busy; it's about effortlessly juggling multiple roles, each with its own set of demands and expectations (many of which we put on ourselves). We want to be the best leaders, moms, partners, and friends. Not only do we tend to be the primary caregivers and take on more responsibilities, but we also carry much more of the mental load. The guilt we feel when we "can't handle it all" or the fear of failure or that we'll make a mistake is high.

The badge of busyness is a testament to our ability to handle it all and take on so much—even at the expense of our own well-being and sense of balance.

It's important to note that what "too busy" looks like will be different for everyone. While my husband and I prefer less-scheduled personal time, we have friends who love a faster pace and are involved in many activities. This isn't about right or wrong but about being self-aware enough to notice whether the way you operate is serving you and your relationships ... or not.

In a world that often equates busyness with importance, it's crucial to pause and ask yourself:

- Is this perpetual busyness truly a sign of success and fulfillment?
- Is this really how I want to live my life?
- What is at the heart of my daily hustle?
- Do I truly enjoy these activities and the pace?
- What is the busyness costing me?

There are many other badges that don't serve us and that we wear without meaning to. The burnout badge. The working-late badge. The pretending-to-be-okay badge. The working-on-vacation badge. Any badge that doesn't align with who you want to be or how you want to feel is NOT a badge to be striving for.

When you're busy being busy, you're missing out on the small joys and opportunities of each day. You're making things harder than they need to be. You're less focused and less productive. You're spending way too much time and energy on what doesn't really matter. And you're stressing out about it all. You're also likely chipping away at your relationships (because the busier we are, the less present we are).

Being too busy hurts our performance. Rest and downtime are necessary if we want to truly be effective and to enjoy our lives. Our minds and bodies weren't designed to be on 24/7. So, it's time to redefine our badges, not by how full our calendars are but by how fulfilling and balanced our lives feel.

SLOW DOWN FOR A MOMENT

Pausing and acknowledging how you're really doing—becoming more self-aware—is the first step to taking back control of your days. In the relentless pursuit of success and busyness, it's easy to forget that clarity—and, along with it, strength and confidence—emerges in our quiet moments of reflection. We must slow down enough to pay attention to where we are struggling and what we really want (or don't want).

We tend to overwork or take on too much when we don't have clarity on what truly matters both in our work and personal lives. We let ourselves get burned out and hurt our health, when our health is what we need the most. We get so caught up in the busyness that we miss out on our life that's happening right in front of us. We miss out on spending quality time and connecting with the people we care about. We don't notice that our thoughts and actions aren't in alignment with who we want to be.

Research shows that experiencing a severe illness or loss often leads people to instantly gain clarity on what matters most in their lives. If you found out today that you had only a year to live, or someone you love had only a short time left, what would you do differently today? Reflecting on this can lead you to figure out what truly matters to you and inspire you to change your ways.

I now know better. But ONLY because I was willing to look at my life and be real with myself. I was willing to look at the areas of my life I was "sucking at" (not being hard on myself, just my way of being real with myself) and decide to do something different.

After that day I shared my reality with Valerie at the daycare, I started to get real about how things were and how I was showing up in my life. Instead of owning my day, I was:

- Working most evenings and weekends, often staying up late or sitting at the kitchen table with my laptop when my kids were hanging out around me
- Checking my emails and responding to messages nonstop and letting everyone else's requests dictate my days (and evenings)
- Scheduling meetings back-to-back and not leaving time to get my own work done during the workday
- Waking up feeling anxious and overwhelmed but not doing anything to ease these feelings
- Having very little energy and patience left for my family at the end of a long day
- Putting everyone else's needs before my own well-being and not giving myself enough "me time".

I thought I was doing what was needed of me. Really, though, I was wearing the busy badge (and many other unhelpful ones) proudly. But this way of approaching my days and my life didn't reflect the leader or parent or partner I wanted to be. I'd lost a bit of who I was in the busyness. Though I'd convinced myself that I was doing things the only way they could be done, what I really wanted was to have more balance in my life. I didn't yet know how to get there, given all the demands.

CONSTANT DEMANDS AND EXPECTATIONS

The expectation in many workplaces is to do (way) more with less. You have requests and notifications coming at all hours of the day. You might feel pressure to keep up with all the demands with too little support. You also see this in your personal life, whether it's how many activities your kids are in or how packed your weekends are.

The reality is that there is never enough time to do everything. The list of tasks, desires, responsibilities, frustrations, and even good things can seem endless, continually outpacing the hours available in the day. This can lead to stress and the feeling that we are always falling behind. Accepting that we cannot do it all—nor should we—is practical and freeing.

That said, the constant demands and expectations coming at you are a reality. In my own research over the years, I've asked leaders and professionals about their biggest challenges when it comes to balance, stress, and being able to perform at their best. A few themes have consistently showed up:

- Not having enough time for all the things to do in a day—make informed decisions, work on projects, send emails, fix issues, exercise, spend time with family, do the laundry, be there for people—it's a lot!
- Looking at everyone else working long hours, thinking you are lazy or not a team player if you want to end the day to go and relax.
- The pace is moving too fast and things keep shifting or are unclear, so it's hard to keep up with all the change and uncertainty.
- Thinking about work when they want to be present with their family OR thinking about personal stuff when they want to be focused at work.
- Always feeling behind and exhausted by the end of the day, and their family gets the worst side of them.
- Feeling frustrated dealing with a difficult colleague or manager and letting that frustration affect their enjoyment at work or personal time.
- Putting too much pressure on themselves and feeling

anxiety about not being able to meet everyone's expectations.
- Constantly doubting themselves, negative self-talk, and not feeling confident speaking up about what they want and need.

Any of this sound familiar? What's the biggest challenge for you? Whatever it is, it doesn't need to stay this way!

You're reading this book because you want to find a better path forward. The demands and expectations aren't going away *and* you have more choice than you realize. But only you can decide to create better balance for yourself. Even the best companies will want to get the most possible out of you.

THE REAL REASON YOU OVERWORK

Want to know the real reason why I believe you keep working more than you want to? Why you aren't making your personal time a priority? Why you put high expectations on yourself yet always feel as if you aren't doing enough? Or why you believe that you need to work harder and put in all those extra hours to be successful? You might think it's because you have no choice. Your job demands it. Your success depends on it. You don't have clarity on what you do want. All of these can be true.

But beneath it all is this: *you care*.

You want to be a strong leader. You want to be a team player. You want to be the best parent and partner and friend you can be. You're a caring person and you strive for excellence. You want to go above and beyond.

These are all noble and great aspirations. The rub is when you strive for these things at the expense of your well-being and what's important to you. This causes higher levels of stress and inner conflict and leads you to take on way more than you can reasonably handle.

Many people assume that they must set aside their own needs to be a leader or move up in their career or even be there for their family. But in doing this, they end up hurting their ability to lead, their performance, and their relationships. It doesn't feel very good to be exhausted or burning out or just surviving each day.

It's great that you care so much. You also need to understand that when you take on too much or you're exhausted, you're not showing up as your best self. And when you take care of yourself, you can then be there for others in a more meaningful way. When you're feeling good and positive, you're more focused, productive, confident, and energetic. When you make what's important to you a priority, you feel more fulfilled and satisfied. When you lead by example, by balancing your drive for achievement with your desire to be present with your family and enjoy your personal time, you start a positive ripple that drives higher levels of performance and satisfaction in others.

YOU DECIDE WHAT BADGE TO WEAR

It's time to choose a new badge—a way of being that is a truer reflection of who you want to be. One that aligns with your values, with what's important to you, with what success looks like and feels like to you.

> **This isn't about being someone you're not. It's about getting closer to the person you really are.**

Again, if you're exhausted and too busy, you can't be the best leader or parent or person you can be. It's that simple. And if you're still thinking, "Well, this all sounds nice, but I can't possibly slow down the pace with my demanding role," or, "I have no choice," I get it. For a long time, I thought that too, so zero judgment.

Here's the thing: you get what you focus on and what you believe is possible. So, if you think you can't, guess what? You'll come up with all the reasons you can't do it, which will influence the actions you take (or don't take)! In the next chapter, we'll explore what's possible and the mindset you'll need to get to where you want to go. But, for now, trust that this kind of change is possible, regardless of your position or circumstance. It doesn't matter if you're an entry-level manager, an executive, an entrepreneur, or just starting out in your career. In any profession, you'll face challenges, stress coming at you, things going wrong, people who frustrate you, and a mile-long to-do list (if you're not careful). You'll stay stuck in the constant state of busyness.

You get to decide what badge to wear. You get to choose who you want to be and how you want to operate. You can choose to *do less* of what you don't want and *do more* of what you do want. This choosing is a continual process of growth and learning about yourself.

The best part? You don't have to change every aspect of your life. Instead, you make a few specific, intentional changes, and these create that positive ripple effect. It all starts with self-awareness and being honest with yourself. Doing so is courageous and bold—and necessary if you want more balance in your life. You can't figure out where to go if you're not willing to look at where you are now.

SELF-AWARENESS IS KEY

Self-awareness is foundational to creating more balance in your life—or to creating any change, for that matter. It's the ability to notice your thoughts, feelings, and behaviours and whether they're helping or hurting you. Often, we get caught up in the actions of the day, going from one thing to the next, not taking the time to stop and ask ourselves questions such as:

- How is what I'm doing helping me or hindering me (or others) right now?
- What are my beliefs about this situation or person and how are these beliefs influencing my actions?
- What am I missing while absorbed in my work and deep in the weeds?
- How could I think about my situation in a better way or take a different action?
- What do I really need right now? What matters most right now?
- What kind of example am I setting for others?

Once you tune in to your habitual thoughts, feelings, and behaviours, you'll start to notice what's feeding them and can then make more mindful choices. You can intentionally choose other ways to view and respond to what's going on rather than just going through the motions or staying caught up in the busyness.

Where are you making easy choices that are making your days harder?

As you become more self-aware, pay attention to what's going on when you make the "easier" choices. As author Jerzy Gregorek says, "Hard choices, easy life. Easy choices, hard life." Every day, you might be making easy choices that are making your days harder. For example:

- Scheduling back-to-back meetings because it's easier to say yes than no to someone

- Avoiding a challenging conversation because it's easier to be quiet than to risk potentially upsetting someone
- Working evenings to keep up because it's easier than a conversation with your manager to reset expectations or inform them that you're making your personal time a priority
- Saying yes to a last-minute request because it's easier than saying you aren't available until tomorrow or need time to recharge
- Taking on a lower-value task that someone else could do because it's easier than delegating.

I'm certain you have some examples of your own. Though doing what's necessary to make your days easier can feel hard, it's also empowering and, in the end, will set you up for more balance, happiness, and success.

You might be thinking, "It's harder for me to choose to stay at work late and miss supper with my family." I challenge you to ask yourself if it's really the harder choice. Could the bold path be going into your manager's office to renegotiate a deadline or communicate that you're going to start leaving work on time? By remaining silent and choosing to miss out on supper, are you taking the easy way out? The answers to these questions will depend on your beliefs, values, and situation. The point is to challenge yourself to be more self-aware and notice these choices instead of staying in auto-pilot mode or avoiding the choices that can help make things better.

STOP GOING THROUGH THE MOTIONS

It's time to let go of habitual ways of living that aren't serving you or aren't aligned with who you want to be, keeping you stuck in the busyness. When I was rushing from work to daycare and back again, just "getting through" each day, I was stuck in unhelpful thoughts and behaviours. These can look like the following:

- Saying yes without considering your current workload and your priorities
- Spending hours tweaking minor details in a presentation
- Assuming that someone is mad at you because you said no to something
- Regularly skipping lunch and breaks, or staying up late to work
- Feeling you need to attend all the meetings, even though you have a capable team
- Checking your phone every few minutes, unable to disconnect and relax
- Being overly critical of yourself
- Having a stressful fifteen minutes every morning trying to get out the door on time
- Beating yourself up at the end of the day for how you handled a situation.

Think of automatic thoughts, feelings, and behaviours as habits of the mind and body. If you ride a bike or drive a car, after a while you can do these things without really thinking about them. Similarly, habitual ways don't need your full attention; they just sort of happen on their own because they've become a regular part of your routine. Your habitual ways are helpful at times, but often they're not. A "Yes, I'll do that!" will come out of your mouth before you've even had a second to think about it!

This doesn't mean being perfect. I still worry about what people think of me, sit at my desk for too long, and am hard on myself at times. Our house gets messier than I'd like and I often cut things a little too close to a deadline. But I do these things way less often than I used to—and with way less stress—and I show up more consistently for what matters to me and who I want to be. No matter the unhelpful habits you want to change, know that it will get easier. At some point, the things that once seemed impossible or hard to do will become part of a regular good day.

By being more self-aware and paying attention to your thoughts, feelings, and actions in the moment, you can stop going through the motions. Once you create space between what's happening and your reaction to it, you can consciously choose a more positive and productive way to respond—one that's aligned with the badge you want to wear.

But without self-awareness, you'll stay stuck going through the motions, caught up in the busyness and rushing from one thing to the next... and out of balance!

CHECK IN: ARE YOU OUT OF BALANCE?

Since you're reading this book, you likely already feel that you're out of balance, but let's check in for a moment. According to the Canadian Mental Health Association, "A moderate amount of stress improves our efficiency and our mental sharpness. But how do you know when your everyday juggling act has stopped being a motivating challenge and has become harmful to your health?" Here are the signs they list:

You feel like you've lost control of your life. This sense of losing control is a common symptom of excessive stress. It suggests that the demands placed on you are outweighing your ability to manage them. There's nothing wrong with you if you can't manage it all—it's simply too much!

You often feel guilty about neglecting your different roles. When overworked or overwhelmed, you may feel as if you can't fulfill all your roles (e.g., worker, parent, partner) effectively, leading to guilt.

You frequently find it difficult to concentrate on the task at hand. Being overloaded leads to higher stress levels, which can impact cognitive functions, making it hard to focus and maintain attention on specific tasks.

You're always tired. Chronic stress and always going, going, going can lead to both mental and physical exhaustion, as the body is in a constant state of heightened alertness.

Be more self-aware and honest with yourself. What rings true for you?

Remember, be kind to yourself and cut yourself some slack— you're juggling a lot right now!

With everything that's expected of you (and that you expect of yourself) in both your work and personal life, it's easy to let the stress take over, take on too much, and end up out of balance. But it doesn't have to stay that way!

What's important is to notice the signs and then choose to make a change, no matter how small. Balance is a daily practice, not a one-and-done goal. It involves making intentional choices every day and constantly adjusting and experimenting. It also involves a willingness to be bold and go against the grain instead of doing what everyone else is doing. To decide to wear a new badge. I promise you that it will become more and more internalized as you do.

In the next few chapters, you'll get clear on your mindset, values, boundaries, and priorities—and how to say no to what matters less. To see more choice available to you that will allow you to step out of the busyness, stop just going through the motions and take back control of your days (and life). As you become more self-aware, you can more easily catch yourself in the moment and make a new choice.

Self-Awareness and Action:
HOW ARE YOU *REALLY* DOING?

Take some time to be honest with yourself about how you're really doing, without judgment. Reflect on these questions and write out freely whatever comes up for you.

- What badge or badges do you wear now?

- What would you say if you stopped to give someone your own "Here's what real life looks like" speech (as I did that day at the daycare)?

- What "easy" choices are you making that are making your days harder?

- Where are you feeling out of balance in your life? What do you now know must shift? What will you no longer settle for? What badge (if any) do you want to wear?

- Where can you cut yourself some slack and also give yourself credit for how you're showing up? (I guarantee you're doing better than you give yourself credit for.)

Be bold. Spend the next few days noticing how your thoughts and actions are helping you or hurting you, without judging yourself. Noticing and being more self-aware is key!

In the next chapter, I'll help you to rethink your time, embrace a new way to work, and instill the beliefs and perspective you'll need to create the balance you want in your life and see it through.

Chapter 2

OWN YOUR TIME, YOUR MINDSET, AND WHAT'S POSSIBLE

"Our society's formula for success and happiness is broken. We think we have to be successful, then we'll be happier, but the reality is it works the other way around."

– Shawn Achor

When I was starting my business after leaving my corporate career, I told a senior leader I wanted to help people to be happy, balanced, and successful. He replied, "It's impossible—you get two out of the three if you're lucky." Though hearing this was slightly deflating, I thought, *Well that's dumb. Why in the world would we settle for two out of three? Why not aspire to it all, or at least play that game and see what's possible?*

I'd already experienced and understood that working less can be more effective. I'll share more about these messy lessons in the following few chapters. And by this point, I also understood the science behind how our happiness and well-being drive our performance and success. To be happier, balanced, and successful—to change the game you're playing and aspire to all three—you'll need to approach your work and the rest of your life in a new way (in a way that works for you). You must also be willing to look at yourself in a new way and bust any limiting beliefs that will hold you back.

During the time in my corporate career when I was working wild hours, I truly believed I HAD to be the one to do everything. One day, I was kindly called out by a more senior leader in a meeting. In this meeting, a question was posed to the group: "Are you an owner or a victim of your workload?" A key aspect of the culture of the company I worked for was being an "owner."

I proudly and confidently declared, "I am an owner!"

I saw myself in that way because I always got everything done, I'd deliver anything asked of me, and I'd go above and beyond. People could *always* count on me to deliver. I even would have told you that I was good at time management because I always hit the deadline (well, almost always). Never mind the fact that I was working long hours and saying yes to everything and everyone.

Which is what this kind leader called me out on, in a room full of my colleagues. "No, Stacey," he said. "You're a victim."

The feedback stung, and it was confusing because I saw myself SO differently. But I also knew it was coming from a good place. I was slowly becoming more self-aware, so I listened and paid attention. He went on to talk about how I always said yes and wasn't owning my workload or commitments. "If you were an owner," he continued, "you'd be more selective about what you say yes and no to and wouldn't just take everything on."

He was right. It was a huge aha moment for me (once the sting settled and I let his words sink in). Back then, I genuinely believed that I had no choice when it came to my workload, that hard work equals success, and that to perform at a high level, I had to prove I could do it all.

THE MESSY LESSON AND KEY SHIFT

I can now, for real, confidently say I own my days. But for many years, I didn't understand that there was a more strategic and effective way to approach work. That we can work less and contribute in a deeper way when we aren't pulled in so many directions. That we can be happy, balanced, and successful. So, just in case you're still in the "this is impossible" camp or believe you have to be the one doing it all, while this isn't an academic book, I offer some science and research in this chapter. This is not just for the "yeah but" types and those who think they have no choice (again, no judgment—I used to be this person), but for everyone. The scientific evidence is to reassure you that a better way is possible and instill new beliefs so you can open up to a new way to do things and see yourself in a new way.

> **We can be happier, balanced, and successful. To do this, we must take ownership of our days and intentionally shift how we think about and approach our work.**

If your work comes at the expense of the other important areas of your life or you feel as if you have to be the one to do it all (at work or at home), you're going to have to shift your beliefs and how you approach your work and your days to create balance in your life. There's no way around this!

When we're exhausted and spread thin, we miss seeing the choices available to us. We more easily slip into a victim mentality and a negative mindset when it comes to our workload and time. We end up being seriously out of balance, saying yes to everything and taking on way too much.

A NEW WAY TO WORK

Let's face it—many people are out of balance because they prioritize work above all else. They desire more flexibility and time to focus on what really matters to them but also feel as though they have no choice. They burn out without even realizing it. They don't see a path to feeling happier, balanced and successful ... YET.

When I was in that planning session on employee engagement results all those years ago, lack of resources and work-life balance were the top two issues (as usual). I remember observing that, on the surface, people seemed to believe that you can't have one without the other—when we have more resources, people would have a better work-life balance. However, if we prioritize work-life balance, we might not have enough resources to do the work (because people would be working less). Resources always seemed to get the focus since the larger conversation was about how could we do more, not less. And resourcing and work-life balance continued to be issues year after year, without really solving either.

In our modern world, it's too easy to let our work seep into the rest of our life. For working parents—especially women, who often juggle more roles and take on more of the mental load—this can lead to even higher burnout, exhaustion, and a bigger struggle to maintain balance. The *Women in the Workplace 2022* report, a comprehensive study conducted jointly by LeanIn.Org and McKinsey & Company, found the following:

- Forty-three percent of women leaders are burned out
- Nearly two-thirds of women under thirty say they'd be more eager to advance in their careers if they could see more senior women leaders able to manage work and life in the way they want to

- Nearly half of women leaders (forty-nine percent) say flexibility is one of the top three considerations when thinking about whether to take a job at a company, or to stay at their current one.

In 2023, the report said, "Women are more ambitious than ever, and workplace flexibility is fueling them. Yet despite some hard-fought gains, women's representation is not keeping pace." Many women are taking steps to prioritize their personal lives—and are also ambitious and want to excel in their careers. The report also highlighted that "men and women see flexibility as a top employee benefit and critical to their company's success."

Thankfully, there is a path forward that can address these common challenges in organizations with the idea that taking care of our well-being and working less makes us *more* effective. You can use your resources more wisely—and not risk losing them!

People want more flexibility, less stress, and a better work-life balance. They are also looking for role models (this could be you)! Ultimately, many clients tell me they just want to do good work, be present with their families, and *feel happier*.

HAPPINESS AND WELL-BEING INCREASES PERFORMANCE

Happiness is a positive emotional state with feelings such as contentment, satisfaction, and joy in our daily lives and experiences. I see my joy and happiness as intertwined—the quiet joy I experience leaves me feeling happy each day. Well-being is a broader concept. It encompasses not only positive emotions but also our relationships, physical and mental health, and our sense of meaning.

Both happiness and well-being are critical drivers of workplace performance. Researchers have found that we're thirty-one percent more productive when our brains are in a positive state. When individuals experience a higher level of well-being, they're more likely to be engaged, creative, resilient, and productive. Companies that prioritize the happiness and well-being of their employees often see a ripple effect of benefits. But this goes so much deeper than typical well-being initiatives, such as Employee Assistance Programs, health and fitness programs, and flexible working arrangements. It involves changing how we approach our work. This is looking at the thoughts, actions, and behaviours that make us more productive at work, happier in our relationships, and more fulfilled at the end of the day.

In his book *The Happiness Advantage: How a Positive Brain Fuels Success in Work and Life*, Shawn Achor writes, "Conventional wisdom holds that if we work hard, we will be more successful, and if we are more successful, then we'll be happy. But recent discoveries in the field of positive psychology have shown this formula is backward: Happiness fuels success, not the other way around. When we are positive, our brains become more engaged, creative, motivated, energetic, productive and resilient at work."

This doesn't mean being positive or happy all the time. That's not realistic. Rather, it's about putting more weight on your happiness.

Happiness is something you create inside you, not something you strive for.

It's not something you attain when you get a promotion or a new house or even when you have the balance you want in your life. It's the result of your perspective in any given moment. It's the result of being present and enjoying the process of working toward your goals and creating the life you want.

Research also suggests that chronic stress contributes to higher levels of anxiety, depression, and hurts our performance. Arianna Huffington, the founder and CEO of Thrive Global, has spoken extensively about the impact of stress and burnout on performance, health, and well-being. She shared, "I wish I could go back and tell myself: *Arianna, your performance will actually improve if you can commit to not only working hard, but also unplugging, recharging and renewing yourself.*"

We've been taught all our lives that more (and more) effort is what's necessary to be successful. This just doesn't seem to be the case.

WORKING LESS MAKES US MORE EFFECTIVE

Emerging research in psychology and neuroscience is challenging the paradigm that working harder equals success, suggesting that working less can, in fact, enhance performance.

The traditional mindset, deeply ingrained in our work culture, is that relentless hard work is the key to achievement. But this approach often leads to burnout, decreased job satisfaction, and reduced productivity—not to mention less happiness. When we have better boundaries and balance between our work and personal life, our performance improves, not only because we feel better, but because we make better decisions around how we spend our time. It's not the hours you spend working but the results you produce that truly matter. Working less helps us to prioritize and focus our efforts in a more effective way.

The law of diminishing returns states that there's a point at which the benefits gained from an activity don't amount to the effort invested in it. In a landmark study by Stanford University, it was found that productivity per hour declines sharply when a person works more than forty to fifty hours a week. After fifty-five hours, productivity drops significantly and putting in more hours is often pointless. Moreover, those working up to seventy hours a week get the same amount done as those who work fifty-five hours.

Mental resources are like muscles that become fatigued after extended use. The brain needs rest to recover and function optimally, just as muscles do. This concept is supported by neuroscientific research indicating that rest, which includes regular breaks and adequate time off, enhances performance and fosters creativity. Detaching from work reduces fatigue and has a positive effect on performance.

Recent studies of the four-day workweek have shown promising results, indicating that this model can lead to higher productivity and performance, better employee morale, and improved work-life balance. A reduced workweek could also look like working thirty-two hours over five days. Studies showed that employees experienced lower stress levels and less burnout, as well as improved physical and mental health. They also found it easier to balance work and personal responsibilities. The reason is straightforward: employees have more time to rest, engage in personal interests, and be with family and friends, all of which contribute to better overall well-being. The employees were also more focused and efficient at work knowing they had extra time for personal activities.

When you put in place stronger boundaries around your work, you start to make better decisions about where to focus your attention and efforts and cut out unnecessary complexity and wasted effort. This research explains how I was able to cut my working hours drastically at the most demanding time in my corporate career and perform even better, although at the time I didn't know the science and was making it up as I went.

Moreover, a reduced-workweek model can be beneficial when it comes to attracting and retaining talent. In today's competitive job market, work-life balance is increasingly valued, and companies that offer a shorter workweek or promote balance are often seen as more attractive employers. This model can be especially appealing to working parents, who face the constant challenge of balancing professional and family responsibilities. That said, I work with many clients who don't have children, and they value their personal time just as much!

You might think you don't (or won't) have enough time for everything, but working smarter, not harder, is of the essence here.

YOU DON'T HAVE A TIME MANAGEMENT PROBLEM

It can be hard to wrap your head around the idea that working less will make you more effective. I get it. You're facing overwhelming pressure every day. People are emailing you at all hours and you're continually asked to do more with less. You have a hard time saying no because you don't want to disappoint anyone and genuinely want to be there for people.

The thing is that your time is valuable and LIMITED. There's only so much of you to go around! So you might think that the solution is getting better at time management.

But here's the truth bomb. Are you ready? Having too little time isn't the problem you need to solve. You don't have a time management problem. *You have a mindset problem.*

Deep down, you might believe that if you just work harder, if you just do "one more thing," if you just keep pushing forward, you'll finally get caught up and THEN you'll feel on top of things. Deep down, you might believe that you'd be selfish or not a team player if you were to make your own time a priority. Deep down, you might believe that it's impossible to keep boundaries and be successful. And these beliefs keep you in the same old patterns and grind. Because our beliefs impact our choices and our outcomes (for better or worse).

So, time management isn't going to save you. Or at least not yet. Until you believe that there is a better way to be successful and that success includes all the parts of your life that matter to you ... or at least until you're willing to let the chips fall where they may and go for it!

Until you adopt a more empowering mindset and beliefs, no amount of time management will fix things.

A more empowering mindset changes how you view and respond to your situation and the actions you take. You start creating meaningful change by shifting your beliefs, which are common thoughts that tend to be ingrained, and making choices that are aligned with the badge you want to wear. When you work from empowering beliefs and ways of being, you're more open to aligning your actions with what's important to you, setting stronger boundaries, and saying 'no' more. But if you believe you have no choice or it's impossible or you have to say yes to everything, your actions and outcomes will reflect this.

You're not alone if you think time management is the problem you need to fix to stop overworking. Or maybe you're naive in the way I was—I thought I was great at time management because I always got things done and hit the deadlines, never mind the fact that I was working at midnight after crushing a full day in the office.

Truly effective time management enables you to work smarter, not harder, so you get more done in less time, even when time is tight and pressures are high. Again, this is about mindset, because if you believe working harder is the answer, you'll struggle to take control of your days and you'll experience more stress.

So before we go any further, let's take some time to get your mindset in order and figure out what beliefs will support creating more balance in your life. Instead of trying to fix everything or implement everything so you can THEN be happy and balanced, we're going to come at it from a different angle. We're going to work on your mindset first.

Once you truly understand that you have a choice, that you get to choose how you think and act, you'll see more possibilities and choices available to you and can take more positive and productive action.

Sometimes, though, we forget about our ability to choose and see a different perspective.

REFRAME YOUR RELATIONSHIP TO TIME AND STRESS

In the midst of our fast-paced, demanding lives, it's easy to feel overwhelmed, stressed out, and as if we have no time. And when we're in this state, we're less likely to see the choices available to us and waste a lot of our time and energy. This isn't about denying the reality of your pressures but about realizing that your reactions to them are within your control. It's about realizing that your time is precious and limited, so you can make better use of it. It's about realizing you can go through your days with more joy, calm, and presence—or you can be frantic, overwhelmed, and distracted. You get to choose.

> **Successful and balanced people experience and value their time differently.**

They are intentional each day. They focus on the values, priorities and consistent daily habits that help them feel and be their best selves.

Reframing your relationship with your time and with stressful situations means shifting how you perceive and interact with them. If you aren't mindful of this, you can slip into unhelpful thinking, which might sound like "I don't have time." "I can't do this." "I'm not good enough." I don't have a choice." You might let out your frustration on your kids when rushing out the door in the morning or resign yourself to blaming your manager for feeling so overwhelmed or letting the stress take over your mood and day. Meanwhile, you aren't doing anything to make the situation better.

Alternatively, you can approach these situations with a more helpful mindset and positive actions. You can reframe your thoughts to: "I have time for what matters." "I can do this." "I'm more than good enough." "I choose to do this." You can take a breather when you're feeling frustrated or say no to someone when you have too much on your plate. These choices can make the difference between a downward spiral, which will make things harder than they need to be, or a more positive, productive path forward.

Worry, frustration, and overwhelm are all normal—we're human after all! But instead of getting pulled into a downward spiral, you can use your emotions as a cue to pay attention and notice if your thoughts and beliefs are helping you or making things worse. You can then choose to think and respond in ways that are more aligned with who you want to be and what really matters to you. Doing so can transform your perspective and reduce the burden of overwhelm and stress. You can reframe "I have to do this" as "I choose to do this." This shift doesn't happen overnight; it requires practice, self-awareness, and mindfulness.

Remember, it's normal to feel overwhelmed, but being too busy isn't a badge of honour or a sign of success. It's a signal that we need to reassess how we're engaging with our life. By actively choosing how we perceive our time and stress, we empower ourselves to lead more balanced, productive, and fulfilling lives.

To do this, you'll need to open yourself up to positive change and believe that a better way is possible in the first place.

YOUR PERSPECTIVE AND BELIEFS SHAPE YOUR REALITY

Have you ever wondered why happiness seems to come easily to some people but is so challenging for others? A person's happiness is largely determined by how they perceive and interpret their experiences and circumstances. This is subjective. Two people can face similar situations but have very different responses to them based on their perspectives. Someone with a mindset oriented toward optimism will typically focus on the positive aspects of a situation, practice gratitude, and seek out solutions and the joy in everyday experiences. As the popular saying goes, "The happiest people don't have the best of everything—they just make the best of everything they have."

Things will go wrong in life. What will bring you happiness is your ability to find gratitude for and positive aspects in even the smallest thing. No matter what's happening around you, a more positive and empowering perspective and path is available to you.

Similarly, your perspective and beliefs about what's possible shape your reality—your experience of everyday life. Your beliefs influence your actions, and your actions influence your outcomes. Here are some of the most common beliefs and actions that hold people back and keep them overworking, overwhelmed, and out of balance:

You believe: "I have to do it all." Or, "I'm a failure if I can't do it all."
So you: Take on too much, scramble to juggle all the big projects at work and get your kids in all the activities, and leave very little time for yourself.

You believe: "I need to be busy to be productive (and I'm lazy if I'm not)."
So you: Spend days, months, maybe even years going, going, going, always on—only to leave yourself run-down, spread thin, and not feeling very productive even though you've put in a lot of effort.

You believe: "I have to work harder and put in long hours at work to be successful."
So you: Continue to overwork and sacrifice your happiness, well-being, and personal time, even though it's hurting your performance and leading to burnout and you're missing out on enjoying your life.

You believe: "I can't take a day off to rest and care for myself or I'll fall behind." Or, "I'm being selfish if I make myself a priority."
So you: Avoid listening to what your mind and body are telling you (you need a break!) even though when you don't take care of yourself, everything feels harder and more stressful.

You believe: "I can do it all on my own." Or, "People will think less of me or believe I'm incapable if I ask for help."
So you: Continue to take on more, go it alone, and don't leverage the help that is there for you (this is especially common for women).

You believe: "I don't have enough time."
So you: Stay in a constant state of feeling behind and overwhelmed, and work even more hours and then be hard on yourself when you don't get everything done (likely because you overcommitted yourself).

These are the very beliefs and actions that are keeping you from what you really want and from feeling in control of your days. Which one sounds most like you? Are there other limiting beliefs that go through your mind? What might be a more empowering perspective?

Here are some examples of perspectives and beliefs that are more empowering.

- "I have time for what matters."
- "I am successful when I balance my work and personal life."
- "Rest and self-care are productive and necessary."
- "Asking for help is a strength, not a weakness."
- "My worth is not defined by how much I accomplish."
- "My time is valuable, and I matter too."
- "My best work comes from a place of calm, not overwhelm."
- "Time off from work is a vital part of professional growth, not a hindrance to it."
- "I define my own version of success."
- "Every step, no matter how small, is progress."

When you become aware of a limiting belief (they will come and we all have them), pay attention. When you're aware of it, you can shift it to an empowering one.

BALANCE BOOSTS PERFORMANCE

Balance isn't just about creating time and space for all the areas in your life important to you. It's about being more present in the everyday moments. When we aren't focusing on the right things at the right time or in a constant state of busyness, we miss out on the small joys and opportunities of each day—moments with our families, our employees, ourselves, our big ideas, and more. And, as we already explored, when you're happier and take care of your well-being, you perform at a higher level. When you work less, you can be *more* effective.

Balance and performance go hand in hand.

This is the essence of what I invite you to step into as you read this book. When we're more balanced, we tend to feel happier and more centered. When our tank is empty, it's way easier to fall into negative thinking and emotions that deplete us even more, and it's hard to feel and show up as our best.

When I used to regularly work evenings and weekends to keep up with my workload, I'd be short on patience with my family and the overwhelm and anxiety would be high. Today, even while running a growing business, juggling family and personal responsibilities, and going through some tougher times personally, for the most part I feel happy, balanced, and successful—my version of success.

You can experience this too—*your* version.

What I want you to take away is that you don't create balance and success in your life by using the latest tools or time management strategies. You create it with an empowering mindset, who you're being, and actions that reflect what truly matters to you. This involves opening yourself up to what's possible and giving yourself permission to create the life you want.

Even if others might do it a different way.

CHANGE THE QUESTION, CHANGE THE GAME

It's healthy to want to be successful in your career AND have space and presence for your family and "me time." To want to work less, feel good, and enjoy your life. To want to be your best self in all your roles. So instead of asking questions such as "How do I get more done in my day?" "How do I achieve more?" or even "How do I slow down?" I invite you to instead ask yourself:

- *How do I want to live my life? How do I want to feel?*
- *How do I want to show up in my life? What kind of leader do I want to be? What kind of parent or partner do I want to be?*
- *What would it look like if I were successful in my work AND had the balance I want in my life?*

When you change the question, you see more choices. Different questions open you up to new ways of thinking about and approaching your days and your life. You change the game you're playing.

To create the change you want to see, you need to have the right mindset and be crystal clear on who you are and what it looks like to operate in a way that works for you. It's too easy to get swept up into the busyness of the day or give up or go down a rabbit hole when you don't yet have this foundation. And it's even easier to look at everyone else and convince yourself you need to do ALL the things they're doing to be successful.

Self-awareness and new beliefs and perspective are what will lead you to meaningful change. You can learn all the tactics in the world, but if you don't have these things, you won't experience the success you want. That doesn't mean you have to wait until you feel "ready". We build this belief and figure things out as we go!

MY CONFESSION

I work with busy teams and leaders who want to create more balance, stress less, and perform at a high level. Here's my confession:

I don't actually care about high performance (stay with me).

Now, I do care about excellence and helping others, but high performance isn't what drives me. When I started to make my own big shift in how I was showing up in my life, I was viewed as a high performer. Even though I was taking on too much and had become a "victim" of my workload, as that kind senior leader pointed out to me, I was still effective in my work (or so I thought). I didn't start making a shift in how I work and show up in my life because I needed or wanted to perform better.

My problem wasn't that I needed to be better at work. My problem was that I felt as though I was missing out on my life.

I didn't want to be working evenings and weekends. I didn't want my family getting the worst side of me. I wanted to be at the kids' weekly swimming lessons or at the lake and not be worrying about a big meeting or what I didn't get done. I wanted to stop feeling as if I were drowning in everything I had to do. I wanted to simply ENJOY my life at a pace that felt right for me. High performance had nothing to do with it.

The same is true today. I'm intentional about doing the things that help me to be (and feel) balanced and happier in my life. I prioritize my personal time, what gives me joy, and my mental health. I take care of myself, especially when life is feeling messy and hard, and create space to focus on my important work. This all helps me to perform better. I tend to get better results the less I work.

That's the paradox. Balance is KEY when it comes to high performance.

This isn't just my opinion and experience. This is hard science. It's a missing piece in terms of the way many leaders and teams are operating these days. It's also the experience of many of my clients and workshop participants who already see themselves as effective at work. For them, being a high performer isn't the main reason for change. They want to be present and their best self with their family. They want to enjoy their personal time. They want to feel happier and more confident in themselves and their choices. And yes, they also want to feel a greater sense of accomplishment in their work.

It's my hope that this chapter helped you start seeing what's possible.

There is a path to working less and enjoying life more. To being more present and patient with the people you care about. To experiencing more happiness each day. To focusing on what really matters instead of being busy, busy, busy and trying to do it all. You will perform even better and lead even stronger when you choose this path. It's up to you to choose it.

It's time to take ownership of your days and life. Step back into the driver's seat. Decide what game you're going to play and develop the mindset you'll need to get you there. One step at a time.

Self-Awareness and Action:
WHAT GAME DO YOU WANT TO PLAY?

Take some time to be honest with yourself about what success looks like to you. Spend some more time to reflect on these questions and write out freely whatever comes up for you.

- How do you want to live your life? How do you want to feel? What do you really want (or don't want)?

- How do you want to show up in your life? Who do you want to be as a leader? As a parent? As a partner?

- What does balance in your life look and feel like for you? What would it look like if you were successful in your work AND had the time and presence that you desire for your personal life and relationships?

- What mindset and beliefs will empower you to create the balance you want in your life? Write out in present tense.
    - » What are the limiting beliefs that come up for you? Write out at least three.
    - » For each limiting belief, write three empowering beliefs.

Be bold. What is the most empowering belief and perspective you can adopt, starting today? Write it on a sticky note and put it where you'll see it often. Repeat this new belief to yourself every single day. It's the reminder and mindset you need to get to where you want to be!

When you're living out of whack with your values, lack boundaries and have a hard time saying no, you'll experience even more stress and struggle unnecessarily. In the next chapter, we'll go deeper into your values and what truly matters to you.

Chapter 3

LIVE AND LEAD WITH YOUR VALUES

"If you know what matters to you, it's easier to commit to change. If you can't identify what matters to you, you won't know when it's being threatened. And in my experience, people only change their ways when what they truly value is threatened."

– Marshall Goldsmith

This is the famous "duck blanket" story in our house. When my son Carter was four years old, bedtime was a battle most nights (if you have kids, you can probably relate). One particular night, my husband was out of town and I was exhausted from the workday and still had a few hours of work to do that evening. Our two-year-old, Emmett, was already asleep, but Carter wouldn't stay in bed.

It felt as if Carter and I went back and forth for hours (it was probably one hour but felt like an eternity). I'd tell him to stay in bed and he'd keep coming out of his room. He had to go to the bathroom or ask me a question. I needed him to get to sleep so I could get back to work. It turned into an angry battle of wills. An adult against a four-year-old! Back and forth. Back and forth.

My patience was *very* thin and the overwhelm was high.

As a last-ditch attempt to get him to stay in his room, I threatened to take away his most special item in the world—his yellow duck blanket—if he left the room again. And guess what? He came out again. So. It. Went. Away. "Forever!" I declared, and to his horror, I took it away. I'm not proud of this and now cringe at how I handled it.

We were both yelling and crying, and I was at my wit's end. I desperately needed Carter to go to bed. And Carter desperately needed my patience and kindness … and for his mom not to be so scary. Eventually, he went to bed, but by this time, I was too wiped to work and the guilt was high and washing over me.

It was a wake-up call. I was seriously out of balance, like a 20 out of 10. My family was getting the worst side of me.

My priorities were out of whack. I valued family and showing kindness, yet I wasn't living in a way that was aligned with these values at all. I wasn't being the parent I wanted to be—because I was exhausted and felt as though I just didn't have anything left to give.

I didn't realize at the time that there was a much better way to handle things and that letting my frustration and overwhelm get the best of me only made the situation so much worse. If you're in a similar situation in which your values are misaligned with your actions, know you're not alone (and you're not a bad parent or person). But it is time to pay attention and make some new choices and take better care of yourself. The thing is, I never would have said that my work was more important than my kids. My actions told a different story.

Thankfully, Carter and I have never had a moment like that again and our relationship is strong. He's fifteen now! (Time really does go by fast).

THE MESSY LESSON AND KEY SHIFT

Back then, I still wasn't self-aware enough to notice or pay attention to how my reactions and stress levels were making my days so much harder to navigate. My behaviour that night with Carter is one of my biggest regrets because it was so out of alignment with my values. That experience also offered me such a valuable lesson: I needed to make my family and myself a higher priority.

> **When we align our actions with our personal values, we experience *less* internal conflict and *more* ease, clarity, and balance within ourselves and our relationships.**

Within a short time, I started to work less and keep boundaries between my work and personal time, get my workload under control, and take better care of myself (somewhat). I became more patient with my loved ones and began to feel more like myself again. My family started to get a better version of me.

When we're behaving in a way that doesn't align with our values, we experience more inner conflict, stress, and guilt. It's so much harder to navigate tougher situations and our relationships are affected. When we're more aware of our values and act in a way that aligns with the person we want to be and what's truly important to us, we experience LESS internal conflict and MORE ease, energy and ... patience.

IMPATIENCE IS A CUE YOU'RE OUT OF BALANCE

When people think about work-life balance, they often think about time. But what about the ripple effect that happens when you're out of balance, such as your impatience with others? I'm not talking about everyday minor frustrations where you keep your cool for the most part. We all get annoyed, frustrated, and impatient at times—again, we're human! I'm talking about frustration that's on another level. Like I felt that night with Carter. There's a ripple effect that happens in your life when you're out of balance, and often it involves being impatient or not present with others. For example:

- Do you stop being kind to others when the pressure is on?
- Are you short on patience or unreasonable at the end of a long day even though you don't mean to be?
- Are you reacting to those everyday frustrations in a way that isn't aligned with your values and the person or leader or parent you want to be, and doing so is making things worse?
- Do you have regrets as you try to go to sleep at night, thinking about how you didn't handle a situation well that day?

If this sounds familiar, know this first and foremost: there is nothing wrong with you. Again, all the stress, frustration, and overwhelm are just hiding your best. It's easy to feel this way when you have too much on your plate, you're exhausted, and you're pulled in too many directions. That's why impatience is often a sign that you're out of balance. It's a cue to pay attention. Your impatience and frustration might also be letting you know that a value is being hit.

My impatience often showed up as a lack of tolerance for delays at work or "problems" with my husband or kids. But I was utterly worn down and wasn't thinking clearly or present in the moment or managing my emotions well back then. I lost perspective.

If we don't judge ourselves and instead look at impatience as a cue to pay attention, we can see that maybe we just need to take some of the pressure off and take better care of ourselves. Our emotions are signals to pay attention and can tell us if something needs to change.

Now when I see or hear someone not showing up as their best, I don't just assume that they're a jerk. I give them the benefit of the doubt and assume that they're super stressed out or their tank is on empty. This isn't an excuse for poor behaviour, of course, but perhaps it can help you approach others and yourself with more understanding and compassion.

Whether you're at the point I was back then or you feel on the edge of it, pay attention. It's time to align your actions with your values and take better care of yourself if you're having a hard time showing up as the person you want to be. It's time to commit to change and make choices that reflect what truly matters to you.

BALANCING FAMILY AND ACHIEVEMENT

Family has always been one of my core values. This value has evolved over time and has come to mean that I am fully present with the people I care about the most. It's the one thing—the most important thing. If I'm giving my best self to my husband and kids, everything else in life feels easier to navigate. And when I'm not, life feels a whole lot harder.

At the same time, perhaps like you, I'm driven and ambitious, and I value achievement in my career. For a long time, these values—family and achievement—were in conflict. Family was my MOST important value, yet my actions showed otherwise. I'd rush through home "duties," and once the kids were in bed, I'd catch up on work tasks. I was pretty good at being optimistic and calm at work, yet I had little patience left when things didn't go smoothly at home. My husband was also overworking back then. We were both spread too thin. My relationships started to suffer.

I'm drawing attention to family and achievement in particular as they're the values that often feel at odds for people. Which leads to this question: Why do we tend to put work first? That reason will be different for different people. It might be because of social norms or a need to provide for your family. Perhaps identifying with your professional role gives you fulfillment, or you have a deep fear of failure. Personally, I just didn't realize that there was a better way. I thought things were what they were and that's just the way it was.

People often say they don't like their job or home life because the pace is too fast or their manager is impossible to work with or they don't feel valued or their kids are difficult. These are all external circumstances. My big shift started to happen only once I looked inward and got clear on what truly mattered to me—not just on what I thought I had to do to be "successful." I looked in the mirror and was honest with myself: I didn't like the life I was living or who I was being.

WHAT ARE YOUR VALUES, EXACTLY?

Your values are what truly matters to YOU. They are fundamental beliefs or principles or ways of being that can guide your behaviour and decision-making. At their essence, they'll be the same in both your professional and personal life. They're different for everyone.

When we live in alignment with our values, we feel happier and more fulfilled. We reduce inner conflict and stress, and we strengthen our relationships. We have more clarity regarding how to act in any given situation.

Getting clear on your values helps you stay on course. It helps you make those tougher choices. If you're the captain of your boat and you find yourself in stormy weather, your values are your compass, guiding you in the right direction.

As Marshall Goldsmith says, "It's easier to make a change if you know that something that truly matters to you is being threatened."

So let's identify your values. Doing so will make it easier for you to work out what you might need to adjust in your life and everyday choices, and what will help you feel more balanced and, ultimately, happier.

Your values

When getting clear on your values, what's important is not just choosing from a list or what you think your values "should" be, but taking the time to reflect on what truly is important to you. Here are some ways to start getting clear on what your values are.

- Reflect on the ways of being that you hold most important.
- Reflect on the times when you felt happiest, most proud, or deeply fulfilled.
- Think about people you admire and respect. Understanding why these individuals stand out can help you pinpoint values that you aspire to.
- Pay attention to situations that elicit strong reactions from you, both positive and negative. Your emotional responses can be indicators of what you value deeply.
- Consider what aspects of your life you wouldn't give up or what lines you wouldn't cross, as these are often tied to your core values.
- Reflect on how you want people to perceive or experience being with you—if someone was giving your eulogy, what would you want them to say about you? This might seem morbid, but it gets to the heart of what you value.
- Reference a general list of values and mark the ones that resonate with you. Then narrow these down until

you have a few top values, say three or four. Finally, reflect on what these mean to you, specifically.

Here are some examples of core values as well as examples of what they might mean to people. Of course, these are only a few examples and each person will have their own interpretation.

- Family: Relationships with the people you care about most
- Honesty: Truthfulness, transparency, and sincerity in all aspects of life
- Connection: Deep and meaningful relationships with others
- Compassion: Empathy, kindness, and concern for others
- Resilience: The ability to recover from setbacks and grow stronger through adversity
- Responsibility: Holding yourself accountable for your actions and commitments
- Courage: The willingness to face fear, uncertainty, or difficulty
- Respect: Treating others with dignity and consideration
- Adventure: New opportunities and play
- Innovation: Change, creativity, and new ideas
- Teamwork: Collaborative efforts and working well with others
- Excellence: High-quality output and attention to detail
- Gratitude: Recognizing and appreciating what you have
- Being present: Fully focusing on your current experience and the people you're with

What else comes to mind for you? These examples are simply meant to get the ideas flowing. Be honest with yourself about what you value most. What's really important to you in your life and behaviors you value? I'll repeat these questions at the end of the chapter. This is just to get you reflecting on your own values.

> For a list of values and other book resources,
> go to **www.staceyolson.ca/balance**.

Get clear on what value is the MOST important to you

The most interesting thing I learned when studying values is that we experience the most conflict when two of our values seem at odds.

As mentioned, for a long time, my top two values—family and achievement—were out of balance, with the latter becoming more intense, important, and time-consuming at the expense of the other. I didn't understand what it meant to live my values, or recognize that there were options available when I faced a conflict between two important areas of my life. I also wasn't focused on what was MOST important to me.

It's common for values to conflict. For instance, the value of financial security, which often leads to choosing higher-paying jobs or working extra hours, might conflict with the value of leisure time. The value of honesty can sometimes clash with the value of maintaining harmony in relationships.

One approach is to consider how you can balance and honour both values. For example, If you were to be honest AND maintain harmony in your relationships, how would you approach the conversation? If you were to be present with your family AND do well in your work, what would you do? Remember, when you change the question, you change the game.

It's also very helpful to be clear on your most important value. If you could only have one, which would it be?

When you do have that tougher decision to make, let your most important value guide you.

Ask yourself in a tougher moment or decision, *What is my number one value?* This can give you instant clarity and confidence regarding how to respond.

Now, my most important value is being fully present with the people I care about. It's my one thing—the most important thing. When I'm present and being my best self with my husband and kids, giving them the right kind of attention and time, everything feels easier. This doesn't just apply to my family, though. When I'm present with my clients or other people, I'm happy with who I'm being. And when I'm not present with the people I care about, life feels a whole lot harder. Having clarity on this value also factored into one of the most important choices I made in my life (I'll talk about this in the chapter on resilience).

LOOK AT YOUR CHOICES THROUGH A VALUES FILTER

Getting clarity on your values is the first step. You must then take actions that reflect these values.

One of the most significant shifts you can make to be more balanced in your life and be the person you want to be is to start viewing your life through a "values filter." This means evaluating your choices and actions, big or small, through the lens of your values. Especially in a moment of conflict.

Ask yourself, *Is this a reflection of who I want to be and what matters most to me?* If it isn't, ask yourself, *How can I behave in a way that is?*

Here are some examples of ways you can align your actions with your values, using them as a filter to guide your choices.

- You value family and balance, but you're staying late at work regularly, which means less time with your partner or kids. You might reconsider your work schedule and delegate tasks to ensure you leave work on time and have quality time at home.

- You value kindness and patience, but you're snapping at your family or colleagues when you're feeling stressed out. You might work on better navigating your stress and taking care of yourself—maybe you try deep breathing, taking short breaks, or stepping away from the situation until you feel calm, to maintain composure and patience.

- You value personal growth and learning, but you often pass up opportunities because you're too busy. You might find ways to integrate learning into your routine, such as listening to podcasts during commutes or scheduling regular, short training sessions.

- You value connection and being present, but you're often checking email and looking at your phone when you're with your team members, family, or friends. You might work on being intentional about putting your phone away when you're with other people.

- You value accomplishment and achievement, but you're taking on too many projects and saying yes to too many things, which leaves you distracted and unfocused. You might work on saying 'no' more so you can focus on your real priorities.

To be clear, aligning your actions with your values does NOT mean being perfect. This is simply a way to help guide your choices. When things get tough or you have a harder decision to make, pause and reflect on your values and the person you want to be, and on how you can act in a way that is a reflection of THAT.

When you align your actions with your values, you show up with integrity. Doing so also creates energy and leaves you feeling more fulfilled. This takes self-awareness and a willingness to be more mindful of your choices, mistakes and all.

Living and leading with your values isn't just about making the best choices for you in the moment—it's about creating a life that is deeply satisfying and meaningful and feels more balanced to you. Alignment with your values reduces the noise of external expectations and focuses your energy on what's genuinely important to you.

Your values may change, and that's okay

It's also important to recognize that your values can shift as you go through different seasons of your life. What you value in your twenties may not be the same as what you value in your forties. It's essential to periodically reassess your values to ensure they still represent who you are and what you want from life.

As your values shift and evolve, you get closer to the essence of who you are and what truly matters to you.

You gain clarity on and wisdom about yourself over time. When I first started on this journey, my top values were *family* and *achievement*. These reflected what was important to me, with family being the most important (even though my actions didn't yet reflect that). Now, those two values have evolved into *being fully present with people* and *excellence in what I do*. I still have high standards and lofty goals in the areas that are important to me. I'm also aware that when I tip into perfectionism, my relationships and my career will be negatively affected.

KEEP YOUR VALUES FRONT AND CENTER

Remember, be kind to yourself. There's nothing wrong with you if you haven't been honouring your values or have been impatient with the people you care about the most. When you're overloaded, it's easy to get caught up in the to-dos, other people's expectations, and what you think you "should" do and lose sight of what truly matters.

When you become more self-aware and more intentional about taking action in a way that reflects your values, you'll notice more quickly when you're off track—and you can more quickly return to making better choices. As you get clearer on your values, I suggest writing them on a sticky note or completing the "one page filter template," which can be found in the book resources. Then review them every single day until they're internalized. I also encourage you to ask yourself this question several times throughout your day: *Is this a reflection of who I want to be and what matters most to me?* If it isn't, ask yourself, *How can I behave in a way that is?* This is how I stay in check and don't get too far off course.

Living and leading with your values will help you to feel more balanced in your life and within yourself. I have witnessed this time and time again with myself and my clients.

When you align your actions with your values, you're not the only one who benefits—you also set a powerful example for your family and team. Leading in alignment with your values creates a culture of authenticity and fulfillment. You see your values reflected (or not) in your version of success, when you're intentional about it. For example, if you finish a project on time and on budget but your team is burned out, is that really success for you? If you excel in your career but miss out on time with family and friends, is that success for you? If you are experiencing financial success but your health is compromised, is that success for you?

Consider your values in any moment and use them to guide your next action, but don't be hard on yourself when you mess up. Use it as an opportunity to grow and reset.

The duck blanket story does have a happy ending. Carter got his blanket back—almost exactly one year later. I was at a neighbour's house, and she was talking about how her teen had a stuffed animal. I asked her, "How do you know when kids are too old for those things?" She responded with wisdom that changed me forever: "Who am I to take away someone else's joy?" It was another huge aha moment for me. I walked home and gave Carter his blanket (which delighted him) and, thankfully, we've never had a fight like that again. Carter still brings it up at times, and we talk about learning from our mistakes. I teach him about forgiveness and how one instance doesn't need to define a person.

Over time, I learned to become more mindful of my thoughts and actions, and I check in with my values. Every. Single. Day. This means asking myself every morning and every night before bed: *Am I showing up in my life the way I want?* When I feel stressed out or overwhelmed, I ask myself: *Is this a reflection of who I want to be?* Most days, these check-ins tell me that I'm happy with how I'm showing up, and when I'm not, I can use this awareness to course-correct quickly. Impatience with my husband and kids now serves as a cue that I likely have too much on the go.

You might still believe you can't possibly do more without compromising your sense of balance and what truly matters to you—that to be successful, you must sacrifice what's important to you or run yourself down. This simply isn't true. It's a choice you're making. And there are other choices available to you.

Both my family and my work are important. And when I do that check-in with myself each day, I'm confident that I'm living my values and that my actions show this to others. I'm also crystal clear on what's MOST important to me—being present with my husband and kids. Because the rest of it doesn't matter without them.

Living and leading with your values is a cornerstone of balance in all aspects of your life. When your decisions and actions are grounded in your core values, you create an internal harmony that ripples through every aspect of your life.

Self-Awareness and Action:
HOW CAN YOU ALIGN YOUR ACTIONS WITH YOUR VALUES?

Take some time to think about these questions and write out freely whatever comes up for you. There are no right or wrong answers, so let go of what you think you "should" write down or what you believe your company or society values. Be open and non-judgmental with yourself.

- What are your top three values—the ways of being that you hold most important?

- How are your values showing up in your work and personal life? Where are your behaviours and actions aligned with your values? Be specific.

- How are your values NOT showing up? Where are your behaviours and actions not aligned with your values? Be specific.

- In what three small ways could you better align your day-to-day choices with your values?

- What do you need to care about less? What isn't aligned with your core values?

- How will you know when you're not in alignment with your values, and how will you get back on track?

Be bold. What is one thing you'll commit to doing this week to better align your actions with your values and what truly matters to you? Write it out, keep it front and center, and check in with yourself often.

Once you're clear on what really matters to you, it's time to look at what's threatening those values. This is where boundaries come in. In the next chapter, I'll share my most embarrassing experience—my "enough is enough" moment and the wake-up call that led me to finally take back control of my days.

Chapter 4

PROTECT YOUR TIME AND ENERGY WITH BOUNDARIES

"Daring to set boundaries is about having the courage to love ourselves, even when we risk disappointing others."

– Brené Brown

One day, shortly after the duck blanket incident, I was at work with back-to-back-*to-back* meetings and I *really* had to go to the bathroom. As usual, I was rushing from one thing to the next and had no free space or buffer in my day. When I finally had a free minute before my next meeting, I rushed into the bathroom stall.

As I sat there, I was checking my email on my phone (I couldn't even give myself a minute to go to the bathroom without squeezing something else in!) and I was thinking about what I needed to do for my next meeting, which started in about ten seconds.

Then my mind started catching up with my body and I thought to myself . . .

Hmmm, something isn't right.

With dread, I realized that I hadn't pulled down my underwear! I'd peed myself. Yes, this well-put-together professional peed herself!

Thankfully, I'm pretty good under pressure. I quickly assessed the situation and breathed a sigh of relief that only my underwear was wet. I cleaned myself up, threw my underwear in the garbage, and went off to the next meeting.

The man I was meeting—an important stakeholder I'd never met in person—was standing right outside the bathroom door waiting for me! I'd thought I'd have a minute to collect myself. Not the case.

So, off we went to our coffee meeting. I played it cool, but—while he was speaking to me—my mind wandered. *Wow*, I thought, while sitting there in my skirt . . . commando . . . *you really think I have my act together. If you only knew what happened ten minutes ago!*

When I finally got back to my desk after a few more meetings, I sat down in my chair and took in the day. I remember this next moment so vividly even as I write this years later. As I sat there, a feeling washed over me—a wave of gratitude moving from the top of my head down my body. I wasn't someone who practiced daily gratitude back then, so it was unusual.

The gratitude feeling came with a big realization: *The distracted person in that bathroom was the same distracted person who was driving my kids around.* I was grateful in that moment that something worse hadn't happened.

And I knew it was time for a change. This was the tipping point and my "enough is enough" moment.

THE MESSY LESSON AND KEY SHIFT

Not only was I fighting with my husband and kids, I was running myself into the ground and making silly mistakes (though peeing myself was by far the most ridiculous). I looked composed on the outside but was a mess on the inside. I don't think people had any idea just how much I was struggling to keep it all together. That day, I decided it was time for drastic change. And so, I put in place a firm, non-negotiable boundary between my work and personal time. I stopped working outside of business hours, *cold turkey.*

I changed the game I was playing by aligning my actions with my values and asking myself: *If I were balanced in my life and effective in my role, what would I do? Well, I certainly wouldn't be working all these hours!* This question helped to guide my choices.

The unexpected thing that happened was that I started to perform even better. The boundary didn't just protect my personal time—sticking to a regular workday forced me to get clear on what really mattered *at work.* I started prioritizing effectively. I learned how to say no. I began to honour what I needed to be effective. I learned how to create space for my own work and still be there for my team and others. I didn't get caught up in frustrations or office drama. I was more productive during the day. I even earned more respect from my colleagues and got a promotion a few months later.

It takes courage and commitment—being bold—to prioritize our own time and well-being. Boundaries protect our time and energy and force us to focus on what really matters and let go of what matters less.

Boundaries can look like saying no to a last-minute request or taking on too much, not responding to emails in the evening, declining social invitations, or distancing ourselves from people who drain us. We might feel guilty or selfish for putting our personal time, needs, or families first. By setting boundaries, we risk disappointing others, but this is often because others have become accustomed to us always saying yes or being available or meeting their unreasonable expectations.

At the busiest time in my corporate career, I made the decision to stop working evenings and weekends. Before this, I'd thought that to set boundaries with my time, I needed to get my workload under control first. I was mistaken.

CARVE OUT YOUR PERSONAL TIME FIRST

When I put that first bold boundary in place to stop working outside of business hours, I thought I'd ultimately tank my career (at this point, I had no idea that balance and high performance go hand in hand). I was regularly working sixty to eighty hours a week when I made this change, and I had no idea how I would manage it all. I just knew I had to be *all in*—I had a bad habit of overworking to break!

Carving out my personal time first with a boundary to end work on time—even though it was counterintuitive—required me to show up differently. Had I waited to get my workload under control first, I would have kept saying yes to way too many things.

I put on a confident face and was feeling nervous about what people would think. I communicated to my leader and important stakeholders that I'd be making my family and personal time a priority and that I'd no longer be working evenings and weekends. I told them I believed I could still be successful with more focus on what was important.

Then, at 5:00 p.m. each day, I forced myself to close my laptop and get out of the office before I could talk myself out of it. I also left my laptop at the office so I wouldn't be tempted to work at home. The goal was to leave work on time and then figure out the rest. I gave myself no wiggle room because I knew I'd cave quickly if I did. I instantly got back twenty hours of personal time in my week.

Once that boundary was in place, I quickly realized that I needed to add another bold boundary to protect my time: a daily two-hour time-block for my own work and to avoid being booked in meetings all day long. I especially needed this time since I'd taken away the option of doing it in the evening. The time-blocks put ten hours of free space back into my work calendar. This meant that I had to be far more selective about what meetings I attended and projects I took on (we'll get to this in the next chapter). Again, boundaries force us to get clear on what really matters and let go of what matters less. With boundaries, you take away the option of trying to be everything for everyone and doing it all.

There will always be more to do

If you're anything like I used to be, you end the day or the week feeling like you didn't do enough. You tell yourself that you could get caught up if you just had a few more hours, even though your to-do list is unreasonable to begin with. You fear you'll be a failure if you can't keep up with it all, and it leaves you more stressed out.

You're also fighting a battle that you'll never win. You'll never get caught up because when you get caught up, there will be more to do! But here's the liberating part—when you accept this reality, it changes how you think about and approach your day. It gets easier to let go and honour your boundaries, instead of constantly fighting to get more done. Yes, it's uncomfortable, but what you're doing now is also uncomfortable.

A LACK OF BOUNDARIES MAKES YOUR DAYS HARDER

Do you find it hard to make time for your personal life or for yourself? Do you find yourself rushing from one thing to the next? Is it hard to leave work at work or even go to the bathroom at times? You're not alone! But without any meaningful boundaries, you'll keep overworking, getting buried in the weeds, doing tasks that you know aren't a good use of your time, and trying to be everything for everyone else. You also teach people how to treat you by what you allow. When you don't set boundaries, people become dependent on you and expect even more out of you. Work and personal requests will keep piling up.

A lack of boundaries prevents you from being your best self and the most effective leader you can be. A leader who has the courage to focus on what's important, not just what's urgent. A leader who takes care of themselves and isn't exhausted and stressed to the max each day. A leader who prioritizes their time and needs, and leads by example. We all can be leaders.

Many employees move up in their organizations because they're seen as people who get things done and can always be counted on. They're the go-to people. They answer the emails and put out all the fires. Everyone looks to them for guidance and knows they'll deliver. But these can be the very things that get in the way of enjoying family and personal time, being strategic and focusing on the right things, and performing at the highest level. It leads to exhaustion and burnout. The looser your boundaries are, the more stressed you will be.

While it was challenging for me to put these boundaries in place, the hardest part was worrying about what other people would think. Overall, I was finding it easier to navigate my days and enjoying the breathing space. While I still felt jam-packed during the workday, I was successfully leaving work on time and no longer working evenings and weekends. Every day I had to tell myself it doesn't matter what other people think at work, what matters is what my husband and kids think.

If you want to be more balanced in your life, you'll need to get better at keeping boundaries and to not be held back by worries about what other people will think.

BOUNDARIES MAKE YOU MORE EFFECTIVE

You likely know you need to stop overworking, say 'no' more, and protect your time better. Maybe you're feeling stressed to the max or cranky with people or at your breaking point. You might still believe that working harder and putting in all those extra hours is what's leading to your stellar performance, and perhaps you fear being unable to keep up with it all. You likely still tell yourself:

- "I have no choice."
- "It's a busy time and will pass."
- "I don't have enough resources."
- "I'm tough enough to push through."
- "People won't think I'm a team player if I make my personal time a priority."
- "I have to do it all."

These simply aren't true. It's time to challenge those limiting beliefs. As you've already learned, working less can make you more effective. Boundaries can make you more effective. Here are a few examples of empowering beliefs regarding boundaries around your time.

- **"My time is valuable."** Recognizing that your time is precious and finite fosters self-respect and ownership of your time. This belief empowers you to prioritize tasks, commitments, and relationships that align with your values, and to say 'no' more.
- **"Setting boundaries protects my energy and is a form of self-care and self-love."** By setting boundaries, you acknowledge the importance of your mental, emotional, and physical well-being.

- **"It's okay to say no."** Understanding that you have the autonomy and agency to decline requests or demands that don't serve your best interests or align with your boundaries or priorities will help you make more empowered choices regarding your time and attention.
- **"Boundaries enable me to feel and be my best."** When you protect your time and energy, you're better able to focus on what truly matters. You'll also feel better. This leads to higher-quality work, deeper relationships, and a more fulfilling life. This belief underscores the idea that boundaries aren't just *protective* but also *productive*.
- **"My boundaries reflect my values and priorities."** Believing that your boundaries are a reflection of your core values and your priorities empowers you to make decisions that are true to who you are. This alignment brings a sense of integrity and purpose to your life.

Boundaries are non-negotiable when it comes to balance and better performance. Remember, people will take as much as you're willing to give, so if you want more balance in your life, it's time to get serious about your boundaries.

> **There will be exceptions, but what do you want your typical day or week to look like?**

As soon as you create a limit, you'll start making better decisions about where to focus your time and attention. Boundaries will help you:

- Align your actions with your values and what matters to you

- Meet your needs to feel and be your best (we waste energy when we don't meet our needs)
- Feel a greater sense of accomplishment in your workday
- Protect your personal time and be more present with your loved ones
- Give your mind and body time to recharge
- Be more focused, productive, and strategic at work
- Allow yourself breathing space in your day.

What else will stronger boundaries make possible for you?

Limits with your time help you focus

Parkinson's law says that a task will increase in (perceived) importance and complexity in relation to the time allotted for its completion. For example, if you're given twenty-four hours to complete a task, the time pressure forces you to focus on execution. You have no choice but to focus on what's essential to get it done or keep it simple (and cut out the distraction and what isn't necessary). If you give yourself a week for the same task, you'll likely spend six days making it a bigger project than it needs to be, or trying to perfect it, or procrastinating.

Now, this doesn't mean you should leave everything until the last minute. This won't set you up well either, as you'll end up scrambling and stressed out. You need to make sure you're giving yourself adequate time to prepare, and breathing space. But understand that work will expand to the time you give it.

This is why boundaries—when you stick to them—will help you use your time more wisely.

YOUR REASON *WHY* MUST BE BIG ENOUGH

Here's the key: the reason why you're setting a boundary (or making any change for that matter) must be important enough to YOU to be worth seeing it through. You must have an emotional connection to your reason why. It needs to be powerful and meaningful to you. It must be bigger than staying with the way things are now. In the last chapter, you explored your values and what really matters to you, so you likely have a better idea of what your reason might be. Remind yourself what's at stake if you don't stick to that boundary!

In other words, instead of just looking at a boundary as something on your schedule—*Leave work at 5:00 p.m.*—connect it to a reason that's deep and personal for you. A reason that will give you the motivation and courage to follow through. My family was my reason. Whenever I felt the urge to stay at work late, I'd remind myself it didn't matter what this VP or that person thought of me. What mattered was what my husband and kids thought of me. This gave me the inner motivation to stick to my boundary.

One client, Kerri, told me that she hated when she didn't feel accomplished in a day. It really, *really* bothered her. When she didn't accomplish what she'd set out to, she'd beat herself up and feel frustrated with others for derailing her day. This was a key insight into her personal values. Only once she connected to her value of accomplishment and what was truly important to her did she give herself permission to block off two hours of uninterrupted focus time during her workday. She had the motivation to protect the time. As a result, she's far more productive and fulfilled, and she feels calmer—and more accomplished most days. She sticks to her boundary because she knows it's key to her success and aligns her actions with her values.

Keep asking "why," each time going deeper until you hit on something that truly matters to you. So, what's your reason to better protect your time and energy? Maybe you want to be a positive example for your team or your kids, to enjoy your personal time, to accomplish your own work, or to simply not feel like crap each day.

WHAT'S A GREAT DAY OR WEEK FOR YOU?

Are you wondering what boundaries would set you up for success? An effective way to figure this out is to reflect on your past good days (or weeks). They'll give you clues as to what works for you. Think about your values and reflect on a great day or week you had (in this stage of your life). Nothing big or amazing had to happen— just a regular day or week that left you feeling good. You may want to use these questions as a starting point.

- When did you get up in the morning?
- What was your morning like?
- What time did you start work?
- What did you do when you got to work?
- What did you feel good about accomplishing?
- When did you have meetings?
- How much free space did you have in your day?
- What time did you leave work?
- Who did you spend time with?
- How did you show up with people?
- What did you do in the evening?
- When did you go to bed?
- Were your days in the week similar to or different from each other?
- What did you NOT do?

Take a few moments, right now, to close your eyes and think about it. Then consider the following questions.

- What boundaries come to mind for you?
- What makes the good days good and what will give you more of them?
- What drains you?
- What will set you up to feel your best?

Next, reflect on what your optimal day or week would look like. If you could have it be the way you wanted, what boundaries would help you to feel and be your best? What will reflect your values and who you want to be? How could you start working toward this vision?

You don't need to implement everything all at once, but considering these questions can help you identify where to start.

Need some ideas? Let's explore some common, effective boundaries regarding time. Keep in mind that there's no one-size-fits-all approach to boundaries. Give yourself permission to do what works for YOU and your life.

For a worksheet on sketching out your optimal day and week, go to www.staceyolson.ca/balance.

EFFECTIVE BOUNDARIES WITH YOUR TIME

Here are a few examples of specific boundaries you could put in place.

Have an end time for work—and leave on time. How many times have you tried unsuccessfully to leave work on time? There always seems to be "one more thing" to do, or what you think will take ten minutes ends up taking an hour, and you still have...one more thing to do! You know you need to get out the door, but you don't, and you feel even more exhausted the next day.

You must have an end time, or work will continue to spill over.

This may sound obvious, but make the decision up front and leave at that time, no matter what. Dismiss the urge to keep working. Expect that this will feel uncomfortable and just do it. Move away from your desk and leave (you can do this if you're working at home, too). Don't give in to negotiating with yourself. You're an adult and perfectly capable of leaving work! If you'd like a little more flexibility depending on the day, give yourself a window to leave work.

You can make it easier to leave by creating some buffer time with no meetings in the last hour of the day or the next morning (this is a boundary), so you can get that "one more thing" done during your work hours. Then leave work on time so you can enjoy your personal life and be rested for the next day.

Add a daily two-hour time-block to your calendar. Once you're keeping a stronger boundary between your work and personal time, you'll quickly realize, as I did, that you need more time during the workday for your own work.

As mentioned, the next boundary I put in place was a daily two-hour "focus" time-block, and I protected it as if it were one of my most important meetings. I needed time to get my own work done because I'd taken away the option of doing it in the evening. I still use this time-block today, and I also set aside longer blocks for deeper work.

When I suggest this to clients, they usually first reply, "There's no way I can block off two hours every day!" But if this is the time you'll be spending on your important work, can you afford not to carve it out? Even if your calendar is jam-packed, if you start putting in a recurring two-hour time-block right now, soon enough, it will start to free up time for you. Use that time to focus on your most important tasks and you'll feel more accomplished.

One of my clients, Sarah, was feeling "scattered, disorganized, unfocused, tired, and as though she didn't have enough time for value-add work." She wanted to focus on projects where she felt she could add the most value instead of fighting fires or being in meetings all day. For four weeks, she added a daily two-hour time-block to her calendar. She quickly felt more in control of her day and had time for value-add work, as well as time to catch up on tasks. She could leave at 5:00 p.m. feeling a sense of accomplishment. Sarah also shared with her team what she was up to, seeking to lead by example. After sticking to that boundary for a month, she told me, "My stress level is lower, I'm more productive, confident, have more peace of mind, and my anxiety went down. It allows for productive time and downtime, brings a calmness to my day, and I follow through more consistently."

All from putting that one boundary in place. Imagine how you'd feel with two hours of focus time each day.

Block off other time during your workday. Putting blocks in your calendar not just for your important tasks and deep work but also for lunch or coffee breaks, a walk, or breathing space between meetings is necessary to protect your time and set you up for success. Even placing strategic time-blocks in your day to respond to emails or notifications (instead of checking messages all day long) can help you be more efficient and less distracted.

Until you get deliberate about creating space in your day for your priorities and needs, you'll keep falling into the trap of being scattered, reactive, and unfocused. We all benefit from space to focus on our important tasks, to think, and to flex when unexpected things happen (and they always do).

Build transition space into your day. Create space to transition between your workday and your home life. All you need is ten or fifteen minutes. This might look like going for a walk, listening to music you love during the drive home, or closing your eyes and taking some deep breaths to release the tension or unfinished to-dos of the day. You could also do this on your way to work after a hectic morning at home. Building this transition time into your day is a boundary. You might already feel pressed for time, but a few minutes to reset can make all the difference. It gives you breathing space and helps you avoid rushing from one thing to the next.

During this time, set an intention around how you want to show up and feel in the next part of your day. These ten or fifteen minutes can change the rest of your day for the better.

Have no-meeting days. Building on the theme of time-blocking, add a no-meeting day to your week, not just for your own focus and productivity but also for that of your team. By setting aside a day where you prioritize your own time and limit distractions, you reduce the stress that comes with a packed schedule and give yourself space for deeper work or to catch up. No-meeting days not only increase focus and productivity—they also help reduce burnout, boost well-being, and promote balance. They provide the space for you to do your best work, without interruptions or distractions.

My personal favourite is no-meeting Mondays. I've had this boundary for a few years and honour it ninety percent of the time. It's been a game-changer for me when it comes to not stressing out about work on the weekends and getting a great start on the week.

Give yourself permission to have "me time" mornings. When you wake up, do you immediately check your phone and respond to emails? Do you sleep late and then feel behind the second you get up? When you're more intentional about your morning, you prime yourself for a more strategic and productive day.

Create a morning routine that allows you space to focus on yourself before you jump into taking care of others or your work. Meditate, go for a walk, enjoy some alone time, journal, practice gratitude, go to the gym, read, set your intentions for the day—do whatever makes you feel good and gives you space for a healthy start to the day. Even fifteen to thirty minutes can make a big difference in how the rest of your day goes.

Today, my boundary is one hour of alone time each morning, and this hour is such an important part of my routine. It's crucial for my sense of balance. Now, this would have been harder for me to do when the kids were younger and not sleeping as well, but again, even thirty minutes of focusing on yourself before anyone else can change your entire day and leave you feeling less overwhelmed, no matter your current circumstances.

To do this, you might need to go to bed earlier, and to be protective about your bedtime, so you feel rested in the morning. I try very hard to be in bed before 10:00 p.m. on weeknights because I value my morning routine so much. This boundary also keeps me from procrastinating about going to bed, which usually involves mindlessly scrolling through my phone then feeling guilty about it.

You can add "me time" to the start of your workday, too. Giving yourself a few minutes to review your priorities for the day or your calendar for the week can be a strategic start to your morning that makes the rest of the day go more smoothly.

Build white space into your calendar. This goes beyond time-blocking for your important work or breaks in your day. White space is extra space. Free, unscheduled space. It's space to pause and reflect, honour what you need to reset, breathe deeply, or simply think through an important task. Instead of scheduling every minute of your day, give yourself moments of white space for more balance, flow, and ease. The more space you give yourself, both at work and at home, instead of scheduling every minute of the day, the more focused and clear you'll be when you're at a meeting or working on an important task or spending time with your kids.

As I reflect on where I'm at right now in my life, spaciousness is even more important to me—and not just in my work. I want more free space during the week to think and process. To read and write. To stay on top of the household and personal tasks. To rest and experience more joy. *More flexibility and less squeeze.*

Let people know what you're up to

When you let people know your boundaries, you don't leave them guessing what's going on. You can communicate your boundaries in a kind and thoughtful way that builds connection, rather than putting up a wall. Focus on what you will (or won't) do instead of telling other people what they can or cannot do. You'll inspire others when you're up front about protecting your time and energy (we'll explore communication in a later chapter on saying no).

ASPIRE FOR STRUCTURE AND FLEXIBILITY

As you reflect on what boundaries will work for you, figure out which ones are non-negotiable (the ones that provide structure) and which are more flexible.

Build your schedule around your non-negotiable boundaries so you're not just hoping and trying to fit them in. Protect the things that you want to happen every day (e.g., working out or leaving work on time) or every week (e.g., a movie night with the family or a no-meeting day). That said, life happens, so give yourself some grace and flexibility where you need, even when it comes to your non-negotiables. It will never be perfect—if you're keeping a boundary eighty or ninety percent of the time, you're doing pretty well.

Flexible boundaries are the ones that you know help you but might be looser, depending on what's happening in your week. Maybe you have a non-negotiable boundary for a maximum number of hours of work in a week (structure) but the hours change day-to-day (flexibility), depending on your workplace.

You might also have to shift your boundaries depending on the season of life you're in. When I got a promotion after I cut my working hours drastically, for a few weeks I was doing my old job and my new one. During this time, I gave myself one hour each night for work if I needed it and prioritized hiring someone to fill my old role. It was temporary, and I quickly got back to my regular workweek.

Again, successful and balanced people think about their time differently and value it more. Think of your boundaries in an empowering way, not in a way that limits you!

You can also set yourself up for success in small ways (e.g., leave your laptop at the office or put your phone away) or creating a "rule" that guides your decisions until it becomes a habit, so you avoid negotiating with yourself; for example, "I'll be home for supper with my family each night," or, "I'll turn my phone off in the evening." You can also have some fun with it—life doesn't need to be so serious. I had one client, Tanya, who set an alarm for 5:00 p.m. every day. When it went off, the song "It's Five O'Clock Somewhere" would play. This helped her leave work on time! If a particular boundary feels too rigid, think about how you can add a bit more flexibility. For example, maybe you leave work between 5:00 and 5:30 p.m. (with 5:30 being the hard end time).

Aspire to have both structure and flexibility in your day. This isn't about being rigid and putting up walls or being perfect. It's about setting yourself up for feeling and being your best, navigating your days with focus and ease, and being okay to adjust when needed. I like to think I'm the most "disciplined undisciplined" person. I show up for what matters and can drop something in a heartbeat when I need more space or feel overwhelmed. On the days when I feel the urge to work late or put in extra hours, I remind myself that I'll be more focused and productive the next day if I end work on time. I'll also be flexible and adjust my boundaries when needed, but that's the exception, not the norm.

Be open to figuring out what works for you and adjusting as needed. Give yourself permission to stop doing it all. And, let people know what you're up to so they understand your boundaries and what you're working on. You don't need to pretend you have it all together!

On the day of my most embarrassing moment, as I was sitting at my desk having that life-changing realization about how distracted I was, a coworker came in. Almost in tears, she told me she was so stressed about a big project and that she was having the worst day. I thought about it for a moment and then decided to tell her. "Well, at least you didn't pee yourself today!"

We had a good laugh, and a few days later, she thanked me for telling her that story because anytime she was having a stressful moment, she'd think of me and feel better—at least she hadn't done THAT. My hope is that you're feeling a little better about yourself, too. And that you're ready to protect your time and energy.

You really can do this!

Self-Awareness and Action:
HOW CAN YOU PROTECT YOUR TIME AND ENERGY?

Take some time to reflect on what boundaries work for you and fit with your life right now. Trust your instincts and let go of getting it perfect. Something is better than nothing! Reflect on these questions and write out freely whatever comes up for you.

- In what areas of your life are you currently good at keeping boundaries with your time? What helps you to honour them?

- What boundaries do you NEED to feel and be your best? How will enforcing stronger boundaries allow you to perform better?

- Considering your values and what sets you up for a great day, what are three new boundaries that would make a difference and that you can put in place? What is your reason "why" for these boundaries? (Knowing this will help you stick to them!)

- What would it look like if you had structure *and* flexibility in your day?

- What can help you stick to your boundaries and set you up for success to follow through? How can you have some fun with it? Who needs to know about them?

- What do you already know you need to take off your plate or care less about so that you can honour your new boundaries?

Be bold. What is the ONE non-negotiable boundary that you can commit to putting in place to better protect your time and energy? Take immediate action!

Boundaries and priorities go together. If you want to be better at prioritizing, you must have stronger boundaries in place. In the next chapter, we'll explore what to focus on so you can work less but contribute in a deeper way.

Chapter 5

GET CLEAR ON YOUR REAL PRIORITIES AND WHAT MATTERS LESS

"Only once you give yourself permission to stop trying to do it all, to stop saying yes to everyone, can you make your highest contribution toward the things that really matter."

– GREG MCKEOWN

A heads-up: If you're reading this book while on vacation, you might want to come back to this chapter later. We're going to be diving into the topic of workload, and reading it might get you into "work brain." Trust your intuition and do what's best for you right now!

On a family trip to Toronto for an NBA game shortly after travel opened up again after the pandemic, my husband, two teenage sons, and I decided to pack only carry-on luggage. We'd usually take a suitcase or two but, for this trip, we wanted to go through the lines at the airport quickly and skip time waiting at baggage claim. We'd have less to tote around the city as we hopped from Ubers to hotels, plus we'd be in control of our luggage (which sounded appealing after hearing so many stories about lost bags at airports at that time). To do this, though, we needed to spend some extra time planning what to pack.

As we were packing our bags, I started thinking about how packing a carry-on is a lot like prioritizing when it comes to our workweek and personal time—or what it should be like.

If you're like many people, your workweek (or life in general) is like an overstuffed fifty-pound suitcase. Maybe even two suitcases! In order to keep up with all the demands and expectations, you end up working even harder and doing more (and more). In other words, you end up packing WAY too much, which leaves you feeling more overwhelmed and slows you down.

Let's say, right now, your workload is an overstuffed suitcase. What if you could take only a carry-on? What would make the cut?

- What do you do that adds the highest value to your team or organization that you want to ensure you have room for?
- What critically important tasks or projects or meetings would you keep?
- What are your strengths? What do you really enjoy and find fulfilling? What do you want to ensure you bring along for the trip (like your favourite sweater)?

More importantly, what would you NOT pack?

- What are the tasks, projects, and meetings that aren't the best use of your time—or a waste of your time?
- What steals your attention from important work or stresses you out that just doesn't make the cut?
- What do you find yourself complaining about, procrastinating on or worrying about? Where are you

getting sucked into drama that you just no longer have room for?

What if you could only pack a carry-on for your life?

- What values, boundaries and true priorities would you ensure you have room for?
- What gives you joy? What important goals or experiences do you want to bring with you? Who are the people you want to have space for?
- Importantly, what doesn't make the cut? What do you no longer have room for?

The reason this analogy works so well is that it requires you to be far more selective and thoughtful about what you say yes and no to. You must ensure you pack what's important. And you must be more willing to let go of what matters less, such as that extra pair of pants (that meeting or event you don't really need to attend even though you want to). Also, consider that if your suitcase is too full, there's no room for anything else—like the unexpected joys and souvenirs.

Everyone wants more time. And the key to having more time is doing less. To be effective, we need space to prioritize, think, and focus on what really matters. This is why boundaries are so crucial. They'll force you to get clear on what's important and let go of what's not. Instead of being spread thin with busywork or drama that slows you down, you'll make better choices about how you spend your time.

When you put it into practice.

THE MESSY LESSON AND KEY SHIFT

I started to own my days and prioritize better once I set boundaries around my work and personal time. I was forced to figure out how to get control of my workload. Again, that's why we start with boundaries. Constraints force you to make better decisions. You take away the option of saying yes to everything. You start delegating and simplifying. We're simply not as effective when we're pulled in too many directions, and we can waste a lot of time being distracted by what doesn't matter as much.

The key to having more time is doing less *and* focusing on the right things. This requires more planning upfront, but it will make your days—and your life—more fulfilling and move the needle on what really matters.

So, boundaries and priorities go hand in hand. The idea of doing less can be a hard concept to wrap your head around, but it can yield dramatic results in your happiness and performance and set you up for that balance you want.

Though you can apply the carry-on analogy to your workdays and your personal life, I invite you to focus first on your workdays if a heavy workload is an issue for you. It's one of the biggest barriers to feeling happier and enjoying your personal time, and one of the biggest contributors to stress levels. It's time to take back control of your days by taking control of your workload!

SOMETHING HAS TO GIVE

Nothing is more deflating than being really busy—wearing your busy badge—and also feeling as if you aren't making any progress. You might be giving it your all, yet work is still seeping into your personal time, projects are taking forever, progress is coming too slowly, and you're feeling stuck. Or you might be doing "fine" but feeling as if you're accomplishing little and not moving forward as much as you'd like on your goals.

We all have an optimal capacity for how much we can reasonably handle, and when we consistently exceed it, we feel overwhelmed and experience diminishing returns from our efforts.

When you already have so much on your plate, saying no to some things can feel a bit scary or impossible. But there is always somewhere you can say no and always a trade-off (more on this in the next chapter). Again, it will take time upfront to prioritize and think through what needs to give, especially if you haven't been doing this and are overloaded. Once you do, you'll more quickly accomplish what's truly important, waste less time on what doesn't matter, and feel more in control of your days. It can then become a regular exercise that helps you stay on course. You can continually check in on your priorities and the to-dos that matter and let go of what matters less. It feels way better than trying to do it all and being overwhelmed all the time.

But first, you have to give yourself permission to do less.

If you're feeling quite overloaded, you'll likely need to make a bigger cut first.

Permission to take some things off your plate granted! If you want to perform at your highest level, focus on the right things, lead at the right level, and be more present and enjoy your life—to live it at a more reasonable pace—this is a necessary step. BUT it's not just about taking things off your plate—it's about making sure you have room for your true priorities. Too often, people say no to the wrong things or don't make room for what moves the needle or for the people who matter.

You may have heard the "big rocks, small rocks, and sand" analogy. If life is a jar, then the big rocks are the most important aspects of it, such as family, health, and where you contribute the highest value in your work, the smaller rocks represent other important but less-critical aspects, and the sand signifies the smallest details and everyday tasks. If you fill your jar with sand first, there's no room for the big rocks. But if you put in the big rocks first, then the small rocks and the sand can fit between them (and some of the small rocks and sand will have to go). We must put the big rocks in first.

When I stopped working so much, started focusing on where I added the highest value, and became honest about my capacity, I had to step back from a few projects and let others handle them. This wasn't easy (I still felt that I had to be on a project, or that I could do it better than someone else), but fewer projects meant fewer meetings and fewer emails. It was easier to step off some projects rather than continue trying to do it all. This created space for me to focus on what was *more* important. Once I made a few cuts, staying focused on the priorities and tasks that mattered felt more manageable and required only regular maintenance.

To that person who's thinking, *There's nothing I can take off my plate*, or, *People rely on me*, or, *We need more staff first*: You can ALWAYS get closer to the heart of what really matters—no matter where you're at now. It involves thinking differently about your time and ensuring you use it more wisely. I still use what I'll share in this chapter monthly, weekly, and even daily, especially when unexpected things happen.

YOUR REAL PRIORITIES

In a world where urgency and importance often blur together, it's easy to treat all tasks as if they hold equal weight. However, the reality is that all tasks are NOT equal. Without getting to the heart of what really matters, you're left unfocused and doing tasks that don't add value or really matter in the grand scheme of things.

The reality is that individuals and organizations often need to manage multiple important tasks or goals simultaneously. The essence of prioritizing still involves making decisions about which tasks or goals are more important than others at any given time.

While it can be tempting to try to do everything or have ten "most important" priorities, research shows that it's far more effective to focus on a small number of priorities. Originally, the word *priority* was meant to be singular. Somewhere in the busy working world, though, the concept of priorities got seriously watered down. This is why some companies often have twenty priorities on their strategic list and why individuals view all the items on their mile-long to-do lists as priorities.

When it comes to high-performance best practices, the common advice is to have no more than three priorities at any given time. Anything more than three is a to-do list, not a priority—confusing the two can lead to decreased productivity and focus. These select few priorities, when consistently nurtured, become the pillars upon which you build steady, meaningful progress, week by week.

Understand that your real priorities are what ideally get more of your time and attention. This isn't just about your work. It's also in your personal life as well. By focusing on your real priorities, you'll find not only a greater sense of accomplishment in your work but also the space to be present with your loved ones and yourself. Of course, you will do more in a day, but the point is that you're clear on your true priorities and focused on what will move the needle with them.

So, what are *your* real priorities?

Where you add the highest value

To figure out your real priorities, start by reflecting on where you add the most value—in your work, your personal life, and your personal growth. What's something of the highest value that only you can do? Consider the unique blend of skills, strengths, goals, and experiences that you bring to the table. What must you ensure you have room for to contribute at your highest level?

In his book *Essentialism: The Disciplined Pursuit of Less* (which I highly recommend), Greg McKeown talks about focusing on what is absolutely essential and eliminating everything that is not. The idea is to concentrate your resources and efforts on a few priorities that will make the most significant impact, rather than spreading yourself too thin over many lesser activities.

In your workplace, this might mean focusing on projects that leverage your specific expertise or that require your voice and contribution most and will create a meaningful positive impact. If you're a formal leader with direct reports, your people are a priority. Similarly, in your personal relationships, there may be roles that are important to you that only you can fulfill, whether as a parent, friend, or family member. It's also crucial to look inward and recognize what you need to do for yourself that no one else can.

In the context of your work, here are some powerful questions to consider.

- Where do you add the highest value to your team or organization or area of focus? Often we think we have to do it all, but we don't. What's the biggest contribution you can make this year or in the next ninety days or quarter?
- Drill down. Keeping in mind where you add the highest value and where you can make the biggest

contribution, what might be your top three priorities in the next ninety days or quarter?
- Again, keeping in mind where you add the highest value and where you can make the biggest contribution, what might be your MOST important priority—the one thing that would make the biggest impact this quarter?
- Looking at your real priorities, what are the three most important tasks for your month, week, and day?
- How can you create more time and space in your day for your real priorities so that you move forward every day on what really matters?
- What do you need to care about less or delegate or say no to that matters less?

First, gain clarity on where you add the highest value and identify your real priorities. Then, when planning your month, week, or day, ensure that your focus and tasks align with these priorities. What specific actions can you focus on this month, this week, and today to make progress on what really matters? As you start to narrow in and focus on these tasks, you'll feel a greater sense of accomplishment each day.

You can ask yourself similar questions about your personal life and for yourself, as well. What works for me is to be clear on where I add the highest value, my top three priorities, and my MOST important priority in these three areas: 1) my work, 2) my personal life, and 3) myself.

Here are some examples of what this looked like during my corporate career as I got clear on my priorities and made changes in my life, and what it looks like for me today.

THEN	Work	Personal Life	Me
Add highest value	Lead team and enhance portfolio management in the organization	My relationships with my husband and kids	
Priorities	Coaching / being there for my team, project portfolio management process improvement, stakeholder/executive relationships and support	Stop working evenings and weekends, be calmer and more patient with my kids and husband, take a family trip	I didn't make intentional time for myself when I first started on this journey, other than my boundaries!
Number one	Leading team and being there for them	Spend quality time and be present with family on evenings and weekends	

NOW	Work	Personal Life	Me
Add highest value	Empowering people to create more balance and presence in their lives and as leaders	Being present and connected with my husband and kids, and people I am with	Being my best self and feeling good
Priorities	The Balanced Leader program and being fully present with coaching clients, spreading the message on social media and speaking, and writing this book!	Being fully present in the small, everyday moments and with people, having unscheduled time in the evenings and on weekends, financial security *and* fun	Having alone time each morning to meditate, walking daily, and thirty-hour workweeks to give myself more space for whatever I want to do
Number one	Writing and marketing this book	My relationship with my husband and kids	Having alone time and space in my day

When I'm looking at my quarter, month, week, or even day, I make sure I'm focusing on these priorities. Again, prioritizing (for real) takes more planning up front but is essential for focus, balance, and high performance. It saves time in the long run.

This focused approach doesn't mean neglecting other responsibilities. You will, of course, have more to do than just those top three priorities. The key is to make sure you have time and space for what really matters and prioritize moving the needle in those areas, which means doing less overall. You'll also have a greater sense of flexibility this way. When unexpected situations arise or when it's necessary to reprioritize, the less-critical activities can be adjusted or dropped.

Keep returning to the carry-on analogy. Take the time to get clear on what you need to pack. And remember, you have other priorities outside of work—this includes you!

But how do you prioritize when there seems to be nothing but conflicting priorities?

A SIMPLE WAY TO PRIORITIZE

How do you know what's important and what's a distraction? Which requests are truly important and urgent and which ones might have to slide or be delegated, negotiated, or ignored entirely? When you're short on time, what do you focus on?

There are many prioritization methods out there (as a quick Google search will reveal), but I like to keep things simple. I use the same strategy at work, at home, and when something unexpected happens. I learned this method when I worked in the project portfolio management world, and it's now what I use in my business, when helping my kids decide what activity they want to do, or when deciding whether I'll clean the house or do something that refills my energy tank in the evening.

When faced with multiple tasks or choices, whether in your professional or personal life, ask yourself this question:

"If I could have only one, which would it be?"

This question might seem basic, but it cuts through the noise and compels you to evaluate what matters most. I know you'll want to do more than one thing, maybe even ten things, but go back to the question. *If you could do or have ONLY one, which would it be?* This tells you what's more important. You can use this question to establish your bigger focus and priorities, to make choices in the everyday moments, or when something unexpected happens and you need to reprioritize your day. Gary Keller also explores this concept in his book *The One Thing: The Surprisingly Simple Truth Behind Extraordinary Results.* He emphasizes the importance of focusing on the single most important task in any given project or aspect of life.

It's natural to want to tackle multiple projects or engage in various activities, but this "one thing" idea forces you to identify what genuinely matters most. It's a tool for making mindful choices that reflect where you can make the most significant impact, identifying what's important and urgent, and enhancing both your effectiveness and fulfillment.

When we're unclear about our real priorities, we may end up saying no to things that really matter, such as a check-in with a team member who's struggling or an important goal or time with family.

For instance, consider a typical scenario at work: you decide that catching up on email is your top task for the day, so you cancel a 1:1 check-in with your direct report. While email can be important, it can also be a distraction. Reading messages doesn't usually result in impactful work or significantly advance your goals.

Of course, your approach should be flexible; there might be days where catching up on emails will indeed be your focus. However, if this starts happening often or at the expense of more important work or being there for people or your personal time, it's worth reassessing to ensure you're focusing on the right things. You might consider creating a time-block for email during the workday.

Get closer to the heart of what really matters

When you're clear on what matters most, in order of priority, it will be easier to shift your focus. For example, one day priority #2 might be more urgent because of a deadline, but the next day, you'll go back to priority #1. Clarity on your priorities will help you better navigate daily choices around what to focus on.

When you have a tougher day or a week where something unexpected happens, you'll drop the things that matter less and focus on what matters most. You get closer to the bullseye, not get further from it. What many people do is drop the things that matter most and get sucked into fires or emails or lower-value tasks that don't truly align with their values, boundaries, and real priorities.

Here's another example. In the evenings, especially on days when your energy is low, it can be helpful to ask yourself, "If I could do only one thing tonight, or in this next hour, what would it be?" Many days I'll step over laundry on the floor to play basketball with my teens (especially since they're at an age where they want to hang out with me less, so this time is even more precious).

If you could get only one thing done today, what would it be? If you could go on only one trip this year, where would you go? If you could only pack A or B, which would you bring? These types of questions keep getting you closer to the heart of what really matters. They can help guide your choices. But what about when you have two important tasks at odds?

Keep coming back to this idea: there can be only ONE most important thing. Many things may be important, but only one can be THE MOST important. If you could have only one, which would it be? This will guide you to what matters most right now.

Once you're clear on your priorities, you'll then need to ensure you have space for them. You must be thoughtful and intentional to ensure you're making progress on where you add the highest value and real priorities.

BE STRATEGIC WITH YOUR TIME

Being strategic with your time means being clear on what really matters and then intentionally focusing on that to make meaningful progress. If you're strategic, you're focusing on the right things at the right time. You're proactive, not reactive—anticipating challenges, expecting the unexpected, and not treating everything as urgent. You're taking full ownership of your days, both the good and the bad. When things get busier, you're paying even more attention to your calendar to ensure you have the space and that you're focusing on the right things.

How else can you be strategic with your time?

Remove your ego from it. The more you put your ego into your workload, the more overloaded and stressed out you'll be. You'll feel the need to be involved in everything and take on way more than you should. When you take the ego out of your work, you'll find it easier to let others do their jobs, which will free you up to do yours. When we tie self-importance to our efforts and involvement, it becomes more challenging to sift out our real priorities—those that are of the highest value.

Be less reactive. Instead of getting caught up in all the noise and distraction and impromptu requests of others, own your attention. It's your responsibility to create space for what matters. It's up to you to say no to a request, tell someone you'll respond to them later, or ask for what you need.

Take something off your plate—now. Again, there's no way around this. The quickest way to relieve some of the pressure and focus on your real priorities is to give yourself permission to take something off your plate. You can delegate or say no or just let go of giving something your attention. This is an obvious one but often the last to happen because we keep trying to do it all.

If you're really overloaded, this will take that bigger cut up front (e.g., stepping off a project or committee) and then maintenance going forward (e.g., not saying yes in the first place). Sometimes, you might even need to put a hold on something important to give it the attention it deserves. Or you might need to acknowledge that you won't ever get to that thing that's been on your to-do list forever and is weighing you down. Let. It. Go. You'll instantly feel lighter.

Keep it simple. This involves stripping away the unnecessary complexity and finding more straightforward ways to accomplish your desired outcomes and tasks. This approach not only saves time and mental energy—it also often leads to more effective solutions. In essence, the pursuit of simplicity is about finding smarter and easier ways to achieve our goals.

A prime example of this is using artificial intelligence to help get certain tasks done more quickly, such as taking minutes in a meeting or summarizing a bunch of data. At work, simplicity could look like automating routine tasks, streamlining communication, having shorter meetings, delegating to others, or just challenging out-of-the-box thinking to find an easier way to accomplish what you want. At home, it could look like finding easy ways to get supper on the table or connect with your partner. Cut out the noise and unnecessary complexity. Let it be easier and take a more straightforward path.

Limit distractions. Identify what typically pulls your focus away from important tasks and find ways to minimize these interruptions. This could involve organizing your workspace, using technology mindfully by turning off notifications, or setting boundaries with colleagues. With fewer distractions, you can complete tasks more efficiently and effectively. The quality of your work will improve, making it easier to meet deadlines and reducing stress and anxiety. Although multitasking is often perceived as a way to be more productive, research suggests that it actually leads to inefficiencies and decreased effectiveness, as it forces the brain to switch tasks repeatedly, costing time and reducing focus. We teach ourselves to be focused or distracted in each moment. Practice being focused instead. That said, we also have to be mindful to be present with people and what comes up in the moment, even if it might be an interruption—it's a balance.

Stick to your boundaries. Boundaries are like your carry-on. They're a must to prioritize better. They'll drive different choices regarding how you spend your time and where you place your attention. You'll be far more effective with boundaries. Go back to the previous chapter and ensure your boundaries offer you space for your priorities and the to-dos that matter. And make sure you have buffers in your calendar and space to flex when unexpected things happen—you know they'll happen.

Say no so you can say yes to what matters more. Saying no is being strategic! You'll need to get a whole lot more comfortable saying no—or delegating or putting pause on things so you can focus on your real priorities. We'll dive into this in the next chapter, as well as what to do with everything that doesn't make the cut.

YES, YOU MIGHT GET PUSHBACK

The reality is that too many people don't have their priorities straight and spend time on the wrong things. Maybe you're a leader whose team members are overloaded and feel as if you don't have anyone you can delegate to. Or perhaps you work with a leader who doesn't support you when you take items off your plate, tracks the hours your bum is in your seat rather than the outcomes that matter, or believes that long hours equate to high performance. Maybe you receive pushback from your leader or a family member for not wanting to do something.

You might get pushback. Don't be surprised and don't let it stop you. If you want to own your days, you, and you alone, must take ownership. Remember, this is YOUR life we're talking about and being as effective as you can be.

Now, this doesn't mean we always get what we want. There are times we might need to adjust our boundaries or temporarily take on something that we don't feel is the best use of our time or the right fit for us.

It's so easy to tell ourselves that we're powerless, or to let fear hold us back to the point that we don't even try to get what we want. We continue in the same old grind. I'm inviting you to open your mind and, regardless of what others are doing, take full ownership of everything within your control.

You have more choice than you realize and you can likely

get away with more than you think. You can also do this in a confident and empowering way. This is the boldness.

And if you do all that you can and you still can't find the right balance in your current environment, then you'll be ready to confidently make the next well-informed decision—whatever that is for you.

Get clear on your real priorities. Have the courage to own your days. You'll perform even better when you do. This takes continual intention and paying attention to the lessons. I still sometimes overcommit, or find my priority tasks colliding, or don't leave enough space in my calendar to prepare. But I'm far better at focusing on the right things, on what moves the needle. And stress way less about it.

You really can do this too!

Self-Awareness and Action:
WHAT WOULD YOU PACK IN YOUR CARRY-ON?

Take some time to have fun with the idea of packing a carry-on for your workload and your life. Reflect on these questions and write out freely whatever comes up for you. Trust your instincts and let go of getting it perfect. Something is better than nothing!

- What if you approached your workweek as if you could take only a carry-on bag? What would you pack? What is the ONE thing you'd make sure you have room for above all else?

- What about for your personal life? What would you take and what relationships do you want to ensure you have room for? What is the ONE thing you'd prioritize above all else?

- What about for you, personally? Yes, you matter too! What do you want to ensure you have space for in your days? What gives you joy and recharges you? What is the ONE thing you'd pack above all else?

- What would you NOT pack? What do you need to care about less? What do you simply no longer have room for, at work and personally? What could you stop doing so you could focus more on your real priorities?

You won't put all your ideas into action at once, but these questions can help you see where you have more opportunity to get clear on your real priorities (and what matters less).

Be bold. What is one thing you can do today to focus on a priority a) in your work, b) in your personal life, and c) for you?

To be able to do less and focus on what really matters, you'll need to say no a whole lot more. Don't worry—you don't have to actually say the word no! In the next chapter, we'll explore how to do this with more confidence and ease, as well as what to do with everything you decided to leave out of your carry-on.

Chapter 6

SAY 'NO' SO YOU CAN SAY 'YES' TO WHAT MATTERS MORE

"We love saying Yes. We find it hard to say No. And it turns out saying a clear and kind No is one of the secrets to a better life."

– Michael Bungay Stanier

My kids have their own styles, especially my son Carter. For four years, he wore shorts every single day—he didn't even own a pair of pants (except for ski pants to go outdoors in our freezing Canadian winters)!

During family photo shoots for weddings or other formal occasions, I'd sometimes hear, "Can you dress your kids better?" My typical response was a no, because we let our kids make their own decisions about their clothes. Sure, I'd encourage them to pick something not stained or ripped, but I wouldn't force them to dress a certain way to please people.

One time, I received a frustrated text message from a family member saying that this was "just an example of how I didn't care about other people and only thought about myself". Because I wasn't willing to make the kids dress up for a photo shoot.

While I silently stuffed down my frustration, Carter asked me what was wrong (kids can tell when something's up). I told him about the text in a matter-of-fact way, explaining that it was just someone's opinion.

He was quiet for a moment and then responded, "Mom, you do care about other people—you care about me and what I want."

Exactly. I exhaled a big sigh of relief and remembered the lesson.

When you say no to something or someone, ideally it's so that you can say yes to something that's more important to you, whether it's to your boundaries, your important work, or your family values. The real priorities. And, as you become better at saying no, there might be frustration and pushback from other people. This is because you're having an impact on what's important to THEM. So don't be surprised. And don't let it hold you back!

At the same time, be careful not to make assumptions about how people will react when you say no or protect your time and energy. One of my most important stakeholders during my corporate career was a fairly intimidating individual. When I put a boundary in place between my work and personal life, I spent some time before our regular check-in thinking about *how* to communicate my new boundary to this person. I told her I'd be making my personal time a priority and no longer be working evenings and weekends. I also shared that I was confident I could still be successful and had already identified unnecessary meetings and tasks that I felt we could remove from our schedules to ensure we were focusing on the right things.

To my surprise, she uttered a sigh of relief. I got the sense that she'd been feeling the grind too, and agreed with my "less is more" approach. Now, it wasn't quite as simple as that. Once we got back into the daily routine, I had to regularly remind her and others about my availability, and I used a variety of ways to communicate what I could and could not do so I could stick to my boundary rather than simply saying no to her requests (more on this later).

Saying no can allow you to honour your values and boundaries, focus on your real priorities, and take better care of your own well-being. That experience with the stakeholder and others at work showed me that we can communicate a no with confidence and in a way that keeps our relationships intact.

THE MESSY LESSON AND KEY SHIFT

We might believe that we have to say yes to all the demands and expectations at work or in our personal lives to keep everyone happy and perform. What holds us back from saying no—and what makes us feel guilty when we do—is often the risk of disappointing or upsetting someone. We don't want to let people down, or we feel guilty when we do. We don't want to be perceived as selfish or not a team player, and we worry that others might think we aren't capable or caring. We don't want to deal with conflict or a harder conversation.

But this is part of the deal. There's a chance that you'll disappoint someone. And this isn't a good enough reason to hold back.

> **Saying no is one of those harder choices that can make your days easier. This isn't about rejecting requests—it's a choice to stay true to your values, boundaries, and priorities.**

Sometimes it's simply about doing what you want to do for no other reason than you want to do it! By learning the skill of saying no, you create the space and opportunity to say yes to what matters more, creating more balance and focus.

As hard as it can be to say no, when we don't, we end up overcommitting, falling out of alignment with our values or boundaries, and missing out on something that matters more to us. So you must be intentional about what you say yes to, and say no a whole lot more.

Even if someone might not like it.

REALLY, IT'S OKAY TO SAY NO

Saying no is an act of self-care and self-respect. But what if you genuinely want to help others as much as you can? What if you take on too much without meaning to? What if you think that saying no will limit your future opportunities? These are common, real-life challenges. I get it. I still experience them.

You must understand that no matter your reasons for saying yes all the time, it's okay to say no and important to do so. You're not a bad person. You're not doing something wrong. When you don't say no, here are some of the impacts:

- Doing things that aren't the best use of your time
- Experiencing a lack of focus (which leads to being distracted and multitasking)
- Losing control over your days and life
- Working more hours than you'd like
- Missing supper or vacation time with your kids
- Taking longer to complete projects that end up being lower quality
- Being spread thin
- Feeling a lack of energy and mental stamina
- Having little or no time to recharge.

If you want balance in your life and to perform at your highest level, it's time to be brave—and bold—about saying no. You're not going to keep doing it all.

Again, you're not a bad person. You don't need to feel guilty.

The key is to ensure you're saying no in support of what really matters to you.

You can communicate your no with confidence and in a thoughtful way that keeps your relationships strong. It can feel counterintuitive in a world that champions the yes, yet the power of a well-placed no cannot be overstated. There's a subtle art to turning down requests or opportunities with grace.

Saying no not only helps you to focus on what matters—it also keeps you from overcommitting and constant overwhelm. This is important because when your plate is overloaded with commitments or you're sacrificing your well-being or values, the true moments that matter tend to slip by unnoticed.

Overcommitting turns up the volume on stress

You know the feeling. The one you get when realize you said yes to something that you *really* didn't want to do. It's that feeling of nervousness in your stomach as you wonder how in the world you'll have time for the new project you just agreed to take on. Or that feeling of resentment you get when you realize you'll have to miss supper with your family or work on the weekend to complete the last-minute request that just came in. You wonder why you keep saying yes to these things when you know that doing so leads to more stress, frustration, resentment—and overwhelm.

Overwhelm typically sets in when the demands on our time and attention exceed our capacity to effectively manage or handle them. And it's not just the quantity of demands that leads to overwhelm and stress, but also their complexity and the pressure around them (e.g., our high expectations or tight deadlines). The feeling of overwhelm and stress can be exacerbated when there's a perceived lack of control over the situation, or when the tasks at hand aren't aligned with our true priorities, boundaries, or values. It's a signal that our mental and emotional resources are stretched thin—and it's a cue that we need to step back, reassess our priorities, delegate tasks, or ask for help. To stop overcommitting yourself.

To say 'no' more!

Sometimes, we'll have to do things that we don't want to do. This is a fact of life. And sometimes, we'll genuinely want to say yes to someone or something even though we already have too much on the go. And sometimes we'll overcommit without meaning to. But to be more balanced in your life—and strategic about your time—you must start to notice the trade-offs and be FAR more mindful of what you decide to say yes and no to.

Adam Grant, the author of many best-selling books, shared this in a social media post: "Balance rarely comes from increasing efficiency. It usually involves reducing responsibilities. The more priorities we have, the harder they are to juggle. It's better to do a few things well than be overwhelmed by many. A key to avoiding burnout is deciding what doesn't matter."

You've already spent time thinking about your values, boundaries, and priorities, so you know where you can say no more. You know what didn't make the cut for your carry-on. Now it's time to use your courage and go for it. To prioritize effectively, it's crucial to get more comfortable with the art of saying no.

You can't wait for someone else to do it for you. If you don't take a stronger stance and have the courage to protect your time and make choices aligned with your values, boundaries, and priorities, you'll continue to stay stuck overworking and overwhelmed.

And remember, if you're stressed out at work, this will affect your home life. If your home life isn't great, your work is affected. It's all connected. It's all your life. So think of saying no as part of creating balance across all the important areas in your life.

Really, it's okay!

YOU'RE ALREADY SAYING NO ALL THE TIME

Decision-making is a fundamental aspect of life. We're constantly making choices. When we decide to spend our time on a particular task, we are, by default, choosing not to spend that time on something else.

For instance, consider the decision to work late hours. When you say yes to working late, you implicitly say no to family time, rest, or personal interests. When you say yes to another project at work and are already at capacity, you're saying no to doing your best work on what you've already been assigned or taking care of your mental health. When you say yes to responding to a work email in the evening, you're saying no to your personal time to disconnect. When you say yes just to make someone else happy (even though you deep down don't want to do it), you're saying no to making yourself happy. When you say yes to going out with friends when you're feeling exhausted, you're saying no to a quiet night at home to recharge. *There is always a trade-off.*

Consider this question posed by Michael Bungay Stanier in his book *The Coaching Habit*: "If you're saying Yes to this, what are you saying No to?"

Understanding and acknowledging the trade-offs is crucial. Doing so brings clarity to our decisions. It empowers us to prioritize. With so many options and opportunities these days, it's easy to get overloaded if you're not careful. There will also be times when two awesome opportunities come up and you'll have to make a tougher choice.

Since you're technically already saying no all the time, I invite you to be more intentional about it. Here's my twist on Stanier's question. I use: *If I say no to this, what am I saying yes to instead?* Asking myself this question helps me to say no from a place of empowerment by focusing on what I am saying yes to instead. I'm a recovering people-pleaser, and I find it much easier to say no when I consider what I am saying yes to that matters more right now. For example, when it comes to family photo shoots, I say no to what other people expect so that I can say yes to supporting my kids' choices about what they wear.

WHAT'S ON YOUR 'NO' LIST?

Writing out a list of what you decide not to do—or what you could potentially not do—helps you see and remember where you can say 'no' more, or delegate, or let go, or delay for now. This can include tasks, behaviours, or commitments that detract from your values, boundaries, and priorities. The great news is that you've already done so much of the heavy lifting by figuring out what matters more and what matters less.

You don't have to get rid of everything all at once (that might be overwhelming!), but there are definitely some tasks you can let go of now. Here are some to consider:

- Important tasks that can be delegated (train someone or let someone else handle)
- Lower-value tasks that can be delegated or stopped altogether
- Regular meetings that aren't productive or don't add value (stop attending or revamp the meeting so it's a more valuable use of time)
- Projects that you've been dragging your feet on or that have been on your to-do list for a long time (confirm that they're real priorities or remove them from your to-do list once and for all)
- Tasks you feel you "should" do
- People who drain your energy (spend less or no time

with them if you can)
- Personal tasks or activities that you can hire others for (e.g., housecleaning), kids' activities (you could limit them to one thing), or tasks you don't enjoy
- Checking email 24/7 or scrolling social media
- What else comes up for you?

Look for a big no to head off numerous small ones

Choosing to say no to a larger project or commitment, even if it's a great opportunity, can be a strategic decision that prevents an accumulation of numerous smaller obligations and responsibilities. When you accept a major project, you're not just committing to the project itself but also to a series of related tasks—meetings, emails, follow-ups, and more. Each of these tasks requires time and attention and, together, they can lead to a cascade of demands on your schedule. By declining the larger commitment or something you really don't want to do, such as a project at work or a school committee, you are, in essence, avoiding many smaller requests. It's a preemptive decision to maintain control over your schedule.

A big no also allows you to maintain focus on your current priorities and responsibilities, ensuring that your time and energy are invested in areas that align with your priorities, boundaries, and values. In short, saying no to a big project is about more than just rejecting a single opportunity; it's about acknowledging and managing the ripple effect of commitments that would have followed.

Say no to the drama

Saying no isn't limited to tasks and meetings. It also includes saying no to engaging in gossip or spending too much time complaining or focusing on what's frustrating you or taking things personally. Drama tends to involve things that are outside our control and consumes a tremendous amount of time, energy, and resources that could be better spent on positive and productive activities. It can drag us down without us even realizing it.

Drama often acts as an emotional drain, diverting our attention from what truly matters and hindering our ability to think clearly and make wise decisions. When we indulge in it, we not only waste our own time but also contribute to a negative environment. By consciously choosing to step away from energy-draining behaviours, we open up more space in our lives. When you start focusing on the right things and keeping boundaries, you'll naturally spend less time in drama (because you'll no longer have room for it).

In essence, letting go of the drama isn't simply about avoiding negativity—it's also about actively choosing to direct our efforts toward what is within our control and what adds value to our lives.

Avoid resentment

One approach that can make it easier to say no, or to determine whether to say no, is to pay attention to your resentment. When channeled correctly, resentment can help you prioritize your needs and communicate your limits. When you feel resentful toward a request or you can anticipate that you'll end up resenting doing it, trust your gut and take this as a powerful cue that what's being asked of you goes against your values, boundaries, priorities, or interests. Remember, saying no is an act of self-care and self-respect. It will help you protect your time, energy, and joy.

Instead of simply saying yes out of a feeling of obligation, pause and check in with yourself about why you feel resentful and about what matters most to you. Use this insight to give you the courage to say no and avoid that resentment OR let the resentment go if you do decide to say yes.

Take a few minutes now or at the end of the chapter to write out everything that you're doing that doesn't align with your values, boundaries, or priorities (what didn't make it in your carry-on), unnecessary drama, and what you feel resentment toward. For each task or responsibility identified, consider whether you can delegate it, delay it, or say no to it altogether. You don't need to get rid of everything at once, but this will give you a list of where to start and what can help to free up your time and attention.

If you're not going to get rid of something, how can you stress less about it or keep it simple? Where do you need to accept that you aren't going to make a change? These days, if I choose to do something inconvenient or not ideal, rather than continue complaining about it (which I admit I can do at times), I reframe to a more empowering perspective. For example, when one kid moved to high school, and the other was still in elementary, I felt it chopped up my day because I had to drive more during the workday. Since I wasn't going to change it, I accepted it and reframed it to: *I will miss this one day when they are no longer around.*

This is all part of making thoughtful decisions to protect your time and what matters more. You can then communicate your decisions in an empowering and caring way.

A CONFIDENT AND THOUGHTFUL NO

A confident "no" is a clear, thoughtful and empowering way to communicate what you are and are not willing to do. The word *no* is often associated with negativity, but in many cases it signals a positive step. To be successful and balanced (whatever that looks like for you), you must focus on what really matters instead of overloading your to-do list and thereby lowering the quality of your work and relationships and increasing your overwhelm and stress. You're saying no for a reason. Time to own this. And not be all weird about it.

Continue to clean up your mindset and limiting beliefs, which we explored in Chapter 2. Often, struggling to say no comes down to thoughts you might not even be aware of—thoughts that are holding you back from communicating effectively. Perhaps you're coming from a place of guilt, comparison, unworthiness, or worrying about what people think and don't even realize that this is what's influencing your actions and keeping you stuck in the grind.

Again, your mindset matters big time. So whenever you need to say no, shift to more empowering thoughts and beliefs. For example: *Saying no to this is the best use of my time and energy*, or, *I show up for what really matters*. Go back to the empowering beliefs you already identified and focus on what you're saying yes to instead.

Grant yourself grace too. It's an ongoing learning process. Keep returning to what matters more to you. Start making tough decisions and real trade-offs. When you take a moment to think about a trade-off, it's easier to feel more confident in what you're saying no to and to deliver this no in a thoughtful way.

Here are ways you can approach saying no with more confidence and ease.

How to communicate a no

If you find it difficult or awkward to say no, how can you communicate your decision in a kind way that keeps your relationships strong? What language inspires confidence instead of chipping away it? Once you have a sense of what to say no to and you feel good about your decision to say yes to what really matters to you, it's time to tackle the question many people struggle with: "How do I say no?" Hint: You don't actually have to say the word *no*!

Pause and create space before responding. This is a great one if your knee-jerk reaction is to say yes. Try, "Let me check my calendar and get back to you." (And then get back to them.) When I first started practicing saying no, I did this often because I wanted so badly to say yes in the moment. It gave me space to think about what I truly wanted and articulate a response. I don't need to do this now, but it served me at the time.

Separate the decision from the relationship. Remind yourself that just because you're saying no to a project or invitation doesn't mean you're disrespecting the person or don't care about them. Keep the decision separate from the person and you'll bring a more positive and caring energy into your conversation, and it makes it easier to follow through.

Focus on the trade-off. This is one of my favourites, and I used this a lot in my corporate career when I first started taking things off my plate: "I can do X or Y—which is more important to you and where I am most valuable?" This is a great one in a work situation where there are conflicting priorities. Help others see the trade-off and let them decide.

Share your reason why (without overexplaining). Let the person requesting something know your reason for saying no in a thoughtful way. For example, "I'd love to take on this opportunity, however, I have a high priority project I am working on right now or I am at capacity . . ." A little context can go a long way (though be mindful not to go into a long justification).

Give an alternative. This is another favourite, especially when it's something I want to do. You don't need to do everything as soon as it's asked of you! If you want to say yes, just not right now, say, "I'm not available tomorrow. I can free up time next week." Or, "I'm unavailable. [This person] from my team can handle it." You can be helpful without taking it on right now.

Use the phrase *Yes . . . and.* If you're asked to do something, you can say, "Yes, I can do that, and what should I prioritize less?" Or, "Yes, I can do that and I can get to it next week." You can avoid using the word *no* by saying something such as this: "I'd very much like to, *and* I'm overcommitted so I'm not able to take on . . ." Avoid saying "Yes, but . . ." which closes down the options.

Focus on the benefit to the other person. If there is a benefit, highlight it. For example, if you don't want to be a bottleneck, the sooner you own your no and communicate it, the sooner the person requesting something can find someone else who can help.

Avoid apologizing. If you consistently say "I'm sorry" when declining requests, you're teaching yourself to feel bad or that you're doing something wrong. You also undermine your confidence and other people's confidence in you. Try saying "Thank you for thinking of me" instead. Remember, it's okay to say no, and there is no need to be weird about it!

Use a positive tone and expression. The emotion behind a message will have a significant effect on how it's received. Be friendly, genuine, and kind when saying no. Acknowledge what they value or express thanks. Positivity broadens people to ideas and options, while negativity narrows vision and creates unnecessary tension. Smiling or expressing gratitude for the opportunity can go a long way.

Have a preemptive conversation to set expectations. As discussed, heading off a big no can save you from having to say numerous smaller ones. For example, when I started to take control of my days, I realized that there were a few projects on my to-do list that didn't align with my real priorities. I communicated that I'd be stepping away and having a team member handle them. I then didn't get the daily emails and requests related to these projects.

Simply say no. You may have heard the expression "No is a complete sentence." The word *no* on its own is a sufficient response, if that's your preference. There's no need for further explanation. That said, I've personally found that including a little context and thoughtfulness in my responses keeps relationships strong, so I use this strategy sparingly.

Here's an email template you can use to communicate a no, weaving in different strategies. Tweak as you see fit!

> Thank you for considering me for this opportunity. [positive tone and express thanks]
>
> I appreciate how important _____ is to you. [positive tone and acknowledge what they value]
>
> I will need to decline this opportunity at this time because _____. [be clear in your no and briefly share your reason]
>
> If you're still looking for someone next _____, I could do it for you then. [give an alternative date]

Or: Yes, I would love to support you on this, and it would mean that _____ would be made a lower priority right now. Which is more important to you? [focus on the trade-off]

Or: It's important to me that we continue to deliver the highest service and quality to you, and with other higher priorities right now, I wouldn't be able to give it my full attention. [acknowledge the benefit to them of your saying no]

Here's how I can support you in a different way. [give an alternative only if you want to]

Thank you for your understanding, and I look forward to our continued partnership. [express gratitude / positive tone and separate the decision from the relationship]

Here are a few other examples of how to say no:

- Thank you for considering me for this opportunity. Unfortunately, I have to decline your request at this time. I appreciate your understanding and wish you the best.
- I appreciate your confidence in me for this project. However, given my current workload, I wouldn't be able to give it the attention it deserves. Can we revisit this once my schedule clears up next month?
- I understand the urgency of our current projects, and I've noticed that the consistent overtime is impacting my effectiveness. I need to stick to regular hours to maintain my productivity and work quality.
- I'm honoured that you thought of me for this request.

I must decline as my schedule is already quite full and we're currently short-staffed. Thank you for considering me.
- Unfortunately, I'm unable to participate due to higher-priority commitments at this time. Thank you for your understanding.

You can apply these strategies when it comes to communicating your boundaries and priorities, which often involves saying no to something or someone to protect your time and energy.

THOUGHTFULLY COMMUNICATE YOUR BOUNDARIES

Once you start to keep boundaries, you'll have to start saying 'no' more. Letting people know what you're up to is an important step to set yourself up for success. Again, boundaries are about what *you* will (or won't) do—they aren't about telling other people what they can or cannot do. You can do this in a confident and thoughtful way with the intention of building connection rather than putting up a wall.

Here are some ways to communicate your boundaries effectively using some of the strategies from above:

- Connect to your reason why and share your boundary with this in mind (e.g., you want to be strategic about your time, maintain your mental health, prioritize your personal time, etc.).
- Don't apologize, and use thoughtful language. You're making an empowered choice.
- Share your reason for the boundary but don't overexplain.
- Look for easy ways to let people know what you're

up to, such as an "I'm unavailable" status with a brief message, or an out-of-office reply, or a note on your door.
- Speak in a positive and confident way rather than in a way that makes it seem as if you're doing something wrong. For example, "I'll respond to this tomorrow" instead of "I can't do this today."
- Keep in mind that you'll likely have to repeat yourself. But the more conversations you have about your boundaries, the more clarity you'll gain on what matters to you.

When I put in place those two boundaries around my time all those years ago—no more working evenings and weekends and a two-hour time-block each day—I told my leader and important stakeholders something along these lines: "I'm prioritizing my family and personal time so will be leaving work on time and won't respond in the evenings unless there's an emergency. I'm confident I can accomplish what's important within the workday and we can still be successful." To my team, I said, "I'll be closing my door to focus for these two hours in the morning and I can be available for you the rest of the day. If it's an emergency, you can come get me. Otherwise, I won't be available during this time. I want you to know that I want to be there for you, and I also need some focus time for my own work. I encourage you to add focus time into your day as well." Sometimes, these statements were met with relief—we could all stop trying to do so much.

Sometimes, they were met with resistance and follow-up conversations were necessary. Stick to your guns and see it through. Also, be open to adjusting where you need to. It might take some time to figure out what works for you and balance making yourself a priority and being there for others.

Pick and choose strategies that feel good for you in your situation when you communicate a no.

For additional resources on saying no and book resources, go to **www.staceyolson.ca/balance**.

Remember, there will always be more to do. If you want to have your version of having it all, you must stop trying to do it all.

Saying no takes both action and practice—and a dose of courage. It can look like declining a request or choosing to delegate something to a team member or telling yourself you're done scrolling your phone for the night. It means being more intentional about your precious time and attention. It does get easier the more you do it. Accept that you might miss out on opportunities. Accept that though people may not like your no, they can still respect you. When you get objections, return to your reason why and follow through or find the courage to have a bigger discussion about your capacity and priorities.

Give yourself permission to say no so that you can say yes to what matters more. Start as small as you need.

Self-Awareness and Action: WHAT WILL YOU SAY NO TO?

Take some time to consider what you want to say no to. Reflect on these questions and write out freely whatever comes up for you. You likely know what you want to say no to, and now it's time to go for it!

- What is something you recently said yes to that you wish you'd said no to? How could you handle the situation differently next time and learn from it?

- What are the tasks and activities (or even people) in your professional and personal life you know you want to say no to more?

- What isn't a good use of your time or drains your energy? What do you need to care less about? What's on your "no" list?

- What's your real challenge when it comes to saying no? Be honest with yourself. This will help you understand what to pay attention to.

- When you need to say no, what's an empowering story or belief you can remind yourself of? When something is requested of you, what can you ask yourself in the moment before committing to it?

- What is something you want to say no to? How could you communicate your no to this in a confident and thoughtful way?

Be bold. What is one thing you can say no to in your work right now? And one thing you can say no to in your personal life right now? Go say no to these two things today! Feel empowered to lighten your load.

When you take back control of your days and focus on what really matters, you'll be more balanced in your life. Remember that the changes don't need to be huge and sweeping. The day-to-day choices can make a big difference, and you don't have to action all your insights at once! Remember, for me this all started with my creating and sticking to one hard boundary, which led to other bold changes and to taking back control of my days.

In the next part of the book, we'll explore how to calm your busy mind, be present, and enjoy your days more. Because creating balance in your life is about more than boundaries, priorities, and saying no. It comes with being more mindful, stepping out of the overwhelm, turning down the volume on worry and guilt, feeling confident in yourself and your choices, and experiencing more joy and less stress. It comes with *feeling* balanced even when life seems crazy.

In the next chapter, we'll look at the power of mindfulness and how to free up your time and mental energy by being more present.

PART 2

Calm Your Busy Mind, Be Present, and Enjoy Your Days More

Chapter 7

BE PRESENT, NOT PERFECT

"Life gives you plenty of time to do whatever you want to do if you stay in the present moment."

– Deepak Chopra

After my "enough is enough" moment and that day in the bathroom, I told myself that if I ever got to the point where I was THAT distracted by my racing mind again, I was done—I'd quit my job. But until then, I'd give it my best attempt to do what I could to take back control of my days.

Thankfully, I didn't quit my corporate career when I first decided to stop overworking and was no longer willing to sacrifice my personal time or my value of family. Because I learned how to keep boundaries, prioritize better, and say no during the most demanding time in my corporate career. Had I just left, I would have taken all my bad habits somewhere else.

I learned that it's possible to work less and accomplish more. I learned that it's much easier to navigate our days when we have space for our work and personal life and are not swept away in the busyness. I learned that we're more effective when we focus on the right things rather than trying to do it all, and that saying no can be an empowering move.

I was working considerably fewer hours, had more time for my family and personal life, and got a promotion. I loved my new leadership role, coaching and supporting my team to be their best selves. I had a stronger voice at the leadership table and really enjoyed the people I was working with each day. Life was much better.

But I was still feeling scattered in my mind and spread thin during the workday. While I had better boundaries between my work and personal time, the pace at work felt nonstop. I was still overwhelmed and constantly worried about what other people thought of me.

One day, about a year after making that big shift, I was in an important meeting at the office. Several of my team members and other leaders and teams in our division were there. I had a significant role to play in the meeting, but all I remember is that I was having a *very* hard time being present. My busy mind was racing. I couldn't focus on whoever was speaking. It's hard to describe the way my mind was jumping all over the place. Sound familiar?

In that meeting I thought, *This is the same feeling as that day in the bathroom—I'm so utterly distracted and can't settle my mind. I swore to myself I'd leave if I ever felt this way again.*

I believed that quitting would be the easiest and quickest way to leave my racing mind behind. But that day, I didn't seriously think that I would. I really did love what I was doing, so it was just a fleeting idea. Or so I thought.

Another perfect storm of change was brewing.

It was also around the time that a senior leader had asked me to consider cancelling my upcoming two-week vacation at the lake because work was too busy. My usual Fridays off were also considered tentative. (After my kids were born, I took Fridays off every summer—and had no problem keeping up with my work because, as you've learned, working less can make us more focused).

I didn't appreciate that my values were being threatened again. Fortunately, I'd already learned my lesson, so I confidently and thoughtfully said no to changing my vacation plans.

While my husband, kids, and I were at the lake on our summer vacation, that voice in my head whispered again, *You're missing your life.* You know the rest: I was thinking about everything going on back at work. And while my mind was distracted, I wasn't present with my family or with my current experience at all.

But I told myself everything would be fine.

Two weeks later, back in the city, I was sitting in the backyard with my husband and jokingly said, "I want to quit my job." Again, I didn't seriously think that I would. Or that he would support this decision to leave.

I'd said this to Kenton over the years, and he'd always talk me out of it because I had a great job at a great company that paid well and where I liked the people—more like I talked myself out of it with his help. And while I'd seriously meant it in the past, this particular day I was genuinely joking when I said it (though I now believe my intuition was guiding me).

"Yes," Kenton replied. "I think you should. You've talked about this enough. Maybe it's time."

I was shocked and surprised and even a little excited. Could I really make such a bold move? Was this truly what I wanted?

I took a week before I said anything to anyone. I made sure I really wanted to leave (and crunched some numbers), and then I gave my two-week notice. I promised myself that I'd follow through no matter what anyone said or what carrots were dangled or what doubts or fears arose in me. It was a surprise to most people. It was a surprise to me!

I wanted to find work that offered more flexibility and fulfillment. I wanted to be more present in my life and to enjoy my days more. I didn't want to feel like I was missing out on my life. What most people didn't realize is that I had NO plan when I left my corporate career. The plan was to figure out a plan!

Most of what I cover in this part of the book is what I learned and experienced after I left my corporate career, though I'm confident that with what I know now, I could go back and thrive in a corporate environment. We waste so much time and mental energy worrying, feeling overwhelmed, and overthinking our every move. And we miss what's happening right in front of us when we aren't present.

THE MESSY LESSON AND KEY SHIFT

We can balance our time, but if our minds are still racing and we can't be mentally present, we won't *feel* balanced. You can keep the best boundaries in the world, but if you're still stressing out about work at home, you won't experience the balance you're looking for. When we aren't present in the moment, we are unfocused, miss seeing the joy, and don't show up with people in a meaningful way.

The times when I was sitting at my desk with my head in my hands feeling so overwhelmed and wondering how I'd possibly get everything done, I wasn't getting done the thing I needed to get done. When I was physically present with my kids on vacation but constantly thinking about work, I wasn't connecting with them or enjoying the experience. When I was in that boardroom but not really hearing others, I wasn't being a strong leader.

As you learn to be more present, you'll free up time and mental energy, strengthen your relationships, and experience less stress.

So many people have no idea just how much energy they expend on worrying about what people will think, feeling guilty, doubting themselves, and running through mental to-do lists. They feel more stressed and experience less joy.

At the heart of being and feeling balanced is the ability to be present in the moment—and in your life.

WHAT'S A BUSY MIND?

Feeling scattered in your head and bouncing from one thought to the next, even while in a meeting or at the supper table? Are you ruminating about that big presentation or the conversation you had yesterday with your manager that didn't go well? Constantly thinking about tomorrow's to-dos while tucking your kids into bed at night or when you're trying to sleep? Feel like your mental health is suffering from all the stress, demands and expectations? These are just a few examples of what it looks like to have a busy mind.

Perhaps you're constantly worried about what other people think or worst-case scenarios. Or you're carrying more of the mental load, keeping track of everything from work to your kids' activities and dentist appointments. Or you simply feel mentally "messy."

If so, you're definitely not alone! All of us experience this to some degree, though some more than others. People's brains function differently—ADHD is one example—which can present unique challenges. However, we all have the ability to tame our busy minds and become more present. Here are some common challenges related to having a busy mind that I hear from clients and have experienced myself:

- Often feeling as if there's something of higher priority or importance or value that you could be doing, which leads to more guilt and doubts
- Constantly worrying about not getting everything on your to-do list done or about what people think of you if you don't

- Losing connection with people when you're with them
- Unable to mentally disconnect from work when you're at home and vice versa
- Being overly critical and hard on yourself (negative self-talk)
- Letting distractions steal your attention from the task at hand
- Physical fatigue and symptoms of burnout, as mental exhaustion often shows up in the body, reducing overall energy levels
- Higher stress levels and missing out on the small joys and opportunities of daily life, with a reduced sense of gratitude and appreciation for the present moment.

At the core of a busy mind is an inability to focus your attention. But stress and distraction have become the norm in our daily lives. Whether it's due to the ping of an email, a notification on social media, worries about tomorrow's meeting, or anxious thoughts about a past conversation, our attention is constantly being pulled away from the present moment. Scattered focus not only diminishes our ability to enjoy life's simple pleasures—it also impacts our mental well-being, productivity, and sense of balance.

A few years ago, while watching my kids' swimming lessons, I was stressing out about a big presentation and wishing I could JUST. BE. PRESENT. I believed this was just the reality of being in a demanding position while having young kids and a busy life.

The truth is that it's not about how busy you are. Being present is a choice. It comes with intention. And some practice!

The mental load you carry

A heavy mental load goes hand in hand with a busy mind. The

mental load that people carry, especially women and moms, is a real thing. It's a significant and underrecognized aspect of our daily lives. Often referred to as the "invisible workload," it encompasses everything from keeping track of appointments and school events to work expectations and ensuring the emotional well-being of our families.

A heavy mental load goes way beyond mere multitasking. It creates an ongoing, relentless cycle of thinking, planning, and worrying about both the logistical and emotional aspects of life and the people we care about. Unchecked, this can lead to chronic stress and burnout. It also hinders our ability to be present and enjoy the everyday moments. By learning to focus our attention and be more present, we can put down some of that mental load (and get better at asking for help).

THE POWER OF MINDFULNESS

To be mindful is to keep your complete attention on what you're experiencing on a moment-to-moment basis, and it requires being aware of your thoughts and feelings in an *open and non-judgmental way*. It's a superpower that you can learn.

When I started practicing mindfulness, I didn't realize just how distracted and NOT present I was most of the time. Our minds can get easily lost in unhelpful thoughts. We lie awake at night because we worry about what might happen tomorrow. Or we can't stop thinking about a mistake we made last week.

When we focus our attention on the present moment—the here and now—we can create a different relationship with our thoughts, feelings, and behaviours. It becomes easier to notice if our thoughts and actions are helping or hurting us. We can see more clearly the choices we're making and feel more confident in the moment that we're choosing what's right for us. We free up time and energy that was previously wasted on worry and guilt and can more easily step out of a downward spiral of anxiety and overwhelm.

Mindfulness offers a way of relating to our days that might be different from what we're used to. It helps us to see that there are different perspectives and ways to view a situation or a person, and to feel more gratitude and appreciation in the moment. Studies have shown that individuals who practice presence and mindfulness experience lower stress levels and increased happiness.

Becoming more mindful will enable you to be more aware of what's stealing your attention and time. It can help you to recognize and appreciate the small joys and accomplishments of everyday life rather than being perpetually caught up in the next task. To let go of the worry about what people think (still a daily practice for me). To be less hard on yourself. To be more focused on the task or conversation at hand. To be present even when life feels chaotic around you.

> **The present moment is all there is, yet we often pay very little attention to it.**

If you're serious about being more balanced in your life (and you are!), it's important to learn how to be more mindful. You'll be able to focus on the task at hand, connect with people more meaningfully, feel calmer and less overwhelmed, stop thinking about work all the time, and more. The good news? Mindfulness is like a muscle—it gets stronger with daily practice (more on this in a moment).

BALANCE YOUR MIND

Mindfulness is a game-changer when it comes to creating balance in your life. A perpetual state of "doing" rather than "being" keeps you focused on the future to-dos, often at the cost of the present moment. This mindset, while common in our society, can lead to a life where moments blend into one another, unappreciated and unnoticed. A quote from Alan Watts that I live by today is, "Stop measuring days by degree of productivity and start experiencing them by degree of presence." But I didn't used to live by this, as you know.

After I left my corporate career (and took some serious downtime), I became fascinated by this question: How do we be our best even with all the demands and expectations coming at us? Because the demands and expectations aren't going away!

This question led me to read a book that changed my life. It opened my eyes to the fact that we have far more choice in where we focus our thoughts and attention than I ever could have imagined. While this idea is ingrained in me now, at the time, it was revolutionary. The book was *The Happiness Advantage: How a Positive Brain Fuels Success in Work and Life*, by Shawn Achor, which I referenced in Chapter 2. I highly recommend it. A big part of the work I do now is a result of this book, as well as my training in positive psychology. It also led me to another book that changed how I saw what was possible with mindfulness and calming my mind: *Choose the Life You Want, The Mindful Way to Happiness*, by Tal Ben-Shahar.

For me, the biggest takeaway of these books was that you experience more of what you focus your attention on. So, the more you focus on the overwhelming thoughts when you feel overwhelmed, the more you feel overwhelmed. When your attention is on worry, the more you worry. When you focus on gratitude and the good things, you see more good. And when you steer your thoughts and attention in a positive and optimistic direction, you're far more likely to create the change you want.

As someone who was a chronic worrier and often distracted by my unhelpful thoughts, this was a big 'aha' for me. You aren't hardwired the way you are. You have the power to focus your attention on the present moment. You have a choice about how you think, and this influences your actions and outcomes. You have the power to train your brain to be more present and focused. And doing so will change your experience of life for the better.

I used to focus on my worry and overwhelm constantly. I was also expending an incredible amount of time, energy, and attention on it, creating more of it and making my days way harder than they needed to be.

Mindfulness opened me up to a whole new way of living. One that's more balanced and peaceful.

MINDFULNESS AND YOUR ATTENTION

There are different elements of mindfulness, with attention and the now—the present moment—being the most foundational one. Attention is the mental process of focusing our awareness on something, whether in your mind or your environment. Think of your attention as a flashlight. You can choose where to shine the beam of light. You can choose to illuminate a specific area, to make it visible. In other words, by focusing your attention on something, you become more aware of what you might not have noticed otherwise.

**The one who chooses where to put your attention—
where to shine the flashlight—is YOU.**

Of all the things that can draw our attention, the present moment tends to receive little of it. Instead, it's more often directed toward the past or the future. We spend a lot of our time and energy worrying about what we did already or what needs to be done.

Thinking and planning are useful and important and have a place in our day. They can also take attention away from what's going on in the moment. By developing the ability to focus your attention on the now, you can free yourself from overthinking and use your mental energy more wisely. It's the practice of being fully present and engaged in the moment, aware of our thoughts and feelings without distraction or judgment. This doesn't mean you won't ever get distracted but, with practice, you'll more easily notice when you do. And when you notice, you can redirect your attention—you can choose where to shine your flashlight.

Other elements of mindfulness

To understand mindfulness, it's important to consider its various elements. These aren't necessarily "types" of mindfulness but rather integral parts of being more mindful and where we focus our attention. They guide how mindfulness can be practiced in the everyday moments.

Awareness of automaticity. When you're aware of your automatic thoughts, feelings, and behaviours, you can create space between what's happening in the moment and your reaction to it. When you're on autopilot and going through the motions, it can be easy to do things without noticing what's serving you and what's not. Mindfulness helps you notice, so you can choose what you want to think, feel, or do next and break unhelpful patterns.

Appreciating the journey toward our goals. Goals are important. Yet focusing excessively on the future (and then being hard on ourselves when we don't hit our goals) leads to more stress and prevents you from recognizing the true value of a present moment.

A mindful approach allows you to enjoy the journey as you strive for goals.

Acceptance. Acceptance means being receptive to allowing an experience or moment to simply occur "as it is". You experience things as they are instead of fighting or resisting them. Acceptance of what is not only frees up energy, but also allows you to move through challenging moments with more ease and less internal conflict.

Self-compassion. Mindfulness involves being kind and understanding toward yourself, especially during difficult times and stressful moments. There's no judgment in compassion, only the realization that bad things happen, that we all make mistakes, and that everyone feels down sometimes. It's a form of acceptance. Being kinder to ourselves is needed for everyone, and it can be especially important for women, who often face unique pressures and expectations.

Non-judgment. Within a fraction of a second, we can form an opinion about someone or something or ourselves. A judgment is like a pair of glasses or a filter . . . a "lens" how we see a person or situation. Mindfulness helps us to be more aware of judgment, so we can judge less and to take other people's judgments less personally. The less judgmental we are of ourselves, the less other people's judgments will hold power over us.

Understanding of self. Mindfulness helps you understand yourself better and make choices that come from within, rather than from external expectations related to your job, others' opinions, or what you think you 'should' do. It recognizes that you are more than your roles and responsibilities, allowing you to cultivate a deeper relationship with yourself and make decisions that reflect your values and authentic self.

Understanding the different elements of mindfulness can help you notice how they show up in your daily life, be more intentional about where you place your attention, and be more present in the everyday moments.

YOUR PRESENCE AND RELATIONSHIPS

It's far too easy to let important people and interactions feel like just one more item on the to-do list, or to miss what's happening in the present moment when we're too wrapped up in our goals. Study after study shows that when people look back at their lives, they regret not making more time for their important relationships or wish they hadn't worked so hard. There's a popular quote on social media right now: "In twenty years, the only people who will remember that you checked your work emails on the weekend will be your kids." This cuts to the heart of the point.

I don't say this to make you feel guilty if you're not spending enough time on your important relationships but to help you recognize the subtle impact we have when we're consistently not present—physically as well as mentally. When you're on your phone while talking to someone. When you're working on your vacation. When you're playing with your kids but checking your email at the same time. Don't underestimate the power of your presence.

Being more present with people can look like the following:

- Putting your phone away when you're with someone
- Giving your full attention to your team member in a 1:1 check-in

- Spending quality time with loved ones each day rather than working more (this can look like being fully present on the drive to school or family supper)
- Being kind and compassionate when someone is frustrating you
- Connecting with others by giving your full attention in a conversation
- Appreciating the moment and joy with the people you want to spend time with.

You never know what tomorrow will bring, so be more present with the people you care about the most today. When you're not focusing your attention on the right things at the right times, you miss out on the small joys of each day—with your spouse, your kids, your team. Even yourself.

Your mind will still wander, and there will be times you'll be distracted when with others. *Be present, not perfect.*

BEING PRESENT TAKES PRACTICE

Mindfulness is a muscle you build. Just like a muscle that grows stronger with regular exercise, mindfulness develops and improves with consistent practice. Keep in mind that mindfulness involves starting over—again and again. You'll get distracted and your mind will wander. This is normal! Especially as you're practicing being present early on. But noticing when your attention is wandering is a good thing. Noticing means you just became present. You can then gently redirect your attention. You'll do this *many* times. Every time you do, you train your attention! And every time you let yourself continue to be distracted, you train your brain to be distracted. It's about awareness.

As your mindfulness muscle grows, you'll be able to withdraw from thoughts about the past or the future more easily when they're not helpful. You'll be able to give your full attention to the step you're taking in the moment or the person you're speaking with instead of the mental burden of one hundred other things.

You'll start to calm your busy mind and experience life more fully. You'll begin to notice the richness of simple moments: the warmth of the sun, the laughter of a colleague, the comfort of a familiar task. Your stress and anxiety will be reduced as you won't be worrying about the future or regretting the past as much. It will enhance your performance, as you'll become more focused and efficient in your tasks. You'll enjoy the journey and each day more, not putting off your happiness until you hit the goal. You'll start valuing your time and energy more, choosing to focus your attention on what truly matters. You'll become more compassionate toward yourself and others, recognizing that perfection is less important than genuine intention and presence.

Embracing the present moment is a continuous practice of bringing yourself back to the now, gently and without judgment. As meditation teacher Sharon Salzberg says, "Mindfulness isn't difficult, we just need to remember to do it."

It's important to note that while many people can benefit from building mindfulness, if you're dealing with higher levels of stress and anxiety, you may require guided support from a professional.

Learning how to be mindful and focus my attention is how I got out of my head, calmed my busy mind, and became more present in my life. When I started building my mindfulness muscle, I found it too uncomfortable to sit down for even five minutes of meditation, so I focused on practicing being fully present when reading a book to my kids at bedtime, doing dishes, and going for a walk.

Being more mindful is what helps me to see more opportunities to say yes or no. It's what helps me to be an effective coach for clients. It's what helps me to have strong connections and relationships with my husband and kids, as well as other people in my life. When I started practicing, I was terrible at it—I had no idea just how *not present* I was until I started to pay attention! Now, it's rare for me not to be fully present with someone or when working on an important task. When you first start building this muscle, you'll likely become aware of just how not present you are—this is normal. And again, the noticing is a good thing.

Right now, you might feel resistance to the concept of building mindfulness. It might feel like one more thing to add to your to-do list. But it actually takes very little energy and can make a really big difference in your life.

Ultimately, it will save you time. Can you really afford not to?

FIVE SIMPLE WAYS TO BUILD YOUR MINDFULNESS MUSCLE

Here are five ways to practice being present and focusing your attention. You can do these anytime, anywhere, and will see the ripple effect in other areas of your life. Pick one and commit to it for the next few days. Spend even just five minutes a day and see the difference for yourself.

Notice where your attention is and move it when needed. This goes back to being self-aware and noticing if your thoughts are helping or hindering you. Notice, but don't dwell on, where your attention is: on guilt, worry, frustration, joy, distraction, pleasure, gratitude, etc. Observe without judging or being hard on yourself. When you notice where your attention is, you become present (this is a good thing).

Then you can choose where to move your flashlight beam, such as to the present moment or a more helpful thought. When you notice your thoughts drifting to past regrets or future anxieties, the key is to gently move your attention back to what's happening right now.

Each time you redirect your focus to the present moment, you strengthen your ability to remain grounded and centered, regardless of external or internal distractions. You may have to do this every couple of minutes. You're training your attention muscle every time you do!

Meditate. There's no right or wrong way to meditate. You might try focusing your attention on your breathing, or you might find a guided meditation helpful. When your mind wanders, consider the thoughts that come up as simply passing events, nothing special. Then gently bring your attention back to the present moment. Try not to focus on concepts or phrases such as *success*, *failure*, *doing really well*, or *try to relax*. Instead, approach your experience with an accepting attitude. In other words, allow it to happen: "This is just how it is, right here, right now."

You can start with five to ten minutes daily at the same time, in the same place, and build from there. Or you can meditate during quiet moments in your day, e.g., when you're washing dishes or taking a walk (this is how I learned to meditate). Again, when your mind drifts (which it will), simply bring your attention back to the moment. Again and again.

Today, I can meditate for thirty to sixty minutes at a time. When I started this practice, five minutes felt like torture. I used to think it wasn't working. It was! It's a practice that helps me be more peaceful in my day. Meditation will help you train your attention and be more present, along with other numerous benefits.

Put focused attention on a routine activity or in conversations. Choose one to three routine activities that you do daily, such as brushing your teeth, putting the kids to bed, having a conversation, eating, doing the dishes, walking your dog, etc. and then, when doing that activity, give it your *full* and focused attention. Pay attention to the smallest detail of what you're doing and what's happening. When your mind wanders, bring it back to the present moment and give the activity your full attention. Even if you have to do this one hundred times. You're training your attention muscle!

As mentioned, when I started practicing being more present, I found it too uncomfortable to sit down for even five minutes of meditation, so I focused on building my mindfulness muscle when reading a book to my kids at bedtime, doing dishes, and going for a walk.

Anchor. In terms of mindfulness, anchoring refers to the practice of focusing your attention on a particular "anchor," or experience, to maintain presence and awareness in the moment. You anchor your attention to something. This could be your breath, a bodily sensation, a sound, or something in your environment, such as the trees or grass. It could be an affirmation or empowering belief. It could be the person you're talking to. It could be a question, such as *What's most important right now?* (from McKeown's book *Essentialism*). The words *right now* are key for anchoring in the present moment.

For example, when I'm getting the kids out the door in the morning and notice I'm thinking about work, I ask myself, *What's most important right now?* The answer is *Get the kids to school*. So, I focus my attention on that—getting the kids to school is the anchor. When I'm focusing on a task and start feeling overwhelmed with thoughts about the other things I need to do, I ask myself that question and return to the task at hand. This builds the muscle of focus.

Anchoring helps you direct your mind back to the present

moment when it wanders. This practice, like the others, helps to develop concentration, reduce reactivity to distractions, and cultivate a deeper sense of calm and awareness.

Practice daily gratitude and self-compassion. Gratitude shifts your attention to the present moment. By recognizing and appreciating what you have here and now and also being good to yourself, you're less likely to get caught up in worries about the future or regrets about the past. You can more easily shift your attention away from the negative thoughts and emotions that often contribute to a busy and anxious mind.

A regular gratitude practice and kindness toward ourselves also increases happiness and positive emotions such as joy, love, and contentment. These emotions can help counterbalance the hectic pace and demands of daily life, providing a calming effect on the mind. As well, gratitude shifts your perspective on challenges. Focusing on what's going well can make problems feel more manageable and less overwhelming.

Incorporating gratitude into your daily routine can involve keeping a gratitude journal, reflecting on positive experiences and wins at the end of the day, or expressing appreciation to others.

The more you practice being mindful, the more natural it becomes, and building this muscle can benefit all areas of your life. The best part is it takes very little energy and you can practice anywhere, anytime, in everyday situations. Remember, catching yourself being distracted is a good thing!

Self-Awareness and Action:
HOW CAN YOU BE MORE PRESENT?

Take some time to reflect on how you can build your mindfulness muscle. Reflect on these questions and write out freely whatever comes up for you.

- How would being more present impact your relationships, performance, and overall sense of balance?

- What common thoughts or distractions typically take away your attention from the present moment? What do you commonly worry about, ruminate on, or overthink?

- Where specifically in your life do you want to be more mindful to focus your attention and be more present?

- Which of these simple practices can you introduce into your life to help be more present and build your mindfulness muscle?

- What will help you remind yourself to be present, not perfect in the everyday moments?

Be bold. Spend the next twenty-four hours being very mindful of where your attention is. Keep moving it back to the present moment. Afterwards, reflect on what you noticed about yourself—what steals your attention? Then keep it up!

Mindfulness will help you to be more self-aware and implement everything we explored in Part 1 of the book with more ease, such as aligning your actions with your values and noticing where to say no more. It will also help you to focus when you find yourself overwhelmed and paralyzed by everything to do, which we will go deeper into next.

Chapter 8

STEP OUT OF THE OVERWHELM

"Overwhelm: When you make the unhelpful decision to stop breathing, lose perspective, and forget you're in control of your life."

– Jen Sincero

There was a period when I used to have one or two panic attacks a week, typically in the morning when I was rushing to get the kids to daycare and myself to an 8:00 a.m. meeting. Most mornings, I'd roll out of bed already feeling anxious about the day, shower, get myself and the kids ready in a frantic, impatient way, and then scramble out the door stressing out about being late. I'd feel overwhelmed with the tight timeline, especially when I had early-morning work meetings.

Often, when we were scrambling to get out the door, I'd be frustrated with my kids for taking too long to do something. My son Emmett would often get frustrated back and things would snowball. He's strong-willed (which I now see as his superpower)—the more I got my back up, the more he'd get his back up! Instead of getting out the door on time, we'd be even further behind. I thought Emmett was just being difficult, but in hindsight, it's clear I didn't handle things calmly or with presence at all.

The panic attacks, which were from an underlying anxiety and came on when I was feeling late to something important, would last only a few minutes but would make the situation so much worse. I'd plow through my overwhelm and keep pushing myself and others out the door instead of taking a five-minute breather. I wouldn't show up calmly or handle my stress well, which made things take even longer and hurt my relationships. Instead of setting a boundary—such as no meetings at 8:00 a.m.—or being mindful of my thoughts or figuring out how to handle the situation better, I let this continue week after week.

When I felt overwhelmed, I'd double down on my efforts and push even harder. I'd put in longer hours and tell myself that when I got all caught up THEN I'd slow down and give myself a break. I'd be unfocused and grumpy with others. This was a stressful way to live—and not very productive after all.

This was what life was like before I learned how to set boundaries and say 'no' more in my corporate career. My impatience and panic attacks were cues that I was seriously out of balance but, back then, I saw them as parts of another day of just getting by and what busy life was like.

When you start to keep better boundaries, take some things off your plate, stop overcommitting yourself, and honour what you need, you can begin to step out of the *constant, daily overwhelm*.

By the time I left my corporate career—while I had learned how to better manage my workload and felt less overwhelmed and more patient daily (with fewer panic attacks)—I had not yet learned how to manage my stress level or how I reacted when the *overwhelm moments* bubbled up. Getting out the door on time was still a super-stressful part of the day—what I now call a "pressure-cooker" moment.

One particular morning, when I was consulting at a new

company, things were snowballing at home in the mornings again. I had an important meeting at 8:00 a.m., was arguing with Emmett about getting out the door, and a panic attack came on. I could barely breathe, I was sobbing, and I had zero perspective on the situation. I dropped Emmett off at daycare still crying (both of us), the guilt high, and then I managed to pull it together and roll into the meeting, pretending that I had it together.

Instead of being present and listening to my mind and body about what I needed or giving myself some buffer in my morning, I kept pushing through to get the kids out the door and myself to work, sacrificing calmness and my connection with my family in the process.

There were also times (often daily) I'd still find myself sitting at my desk feeling paralyzed, thinking that I didn't have time for everything I had to do, never mind the fact that I wasn't getting done the things I needed to get done. Or managing the logistics of daily life, from school runs to work meetings, I was still rushing from one thing to the next and not yet slowing down to appreciate the moment in front of me.

What I really needed was to slow it down, get some perspective, and step out of the overwhelm, which thankfully I can do pretty well these days. You can step out of your overwhelm too!

THE MESSY LESSON AND KEY SHIFT

Overwhelm is something we all experience. We get caught up focusing our attention on all the things we need to do, stress ramps up and we end up being less productive. We forget that we do in fact have a choice about what we say yes to and that we're the ones in control of our days. We lose perspective and forget we have the ability to remain calm.

When we slow it down and pay attention to what we need, or

focus on one thing instead of ten things or handle the pressure cooker moments better, we can be overwhelmed for a few minutes at a time instead of all day, day after day.

When you feel overwhelmed, slow down and do less instead of plowing through.

When demands on our time and attention come faster than we can manage, we lose a sense of control and more easily become overwhelmed. This state of overwhelm not only reduces our focus and productivity but also doesn't feel very good.

It's far more effective to address overwhelm in the moment by honouring what we need rather than pushing forward—even though it feels counterintuitive when you have lots to do. This is another huge lesson that changed my life.

Today, when the overwhelm settles in or a panic attack starts brewing (it can still come up when I feel late for something important), I pay attention to the cues and then slow things down. I breathe. I focus on what matters most in the moment or what I need. I catch myself before it snowballs.

When overwhelm bubbles up, I now do the exact opposite of what I used to do. How balanced you feel is directly proportional to how well you can handle your overwhelm.

YOU CAN BE OVERWHELMED OR CALM— YOU GET TO CHOOSE

People often feel overwhelmed when they need to make a big decision, something unexpected happens in their day, or they have too much to do. But these things are a part of life. We all have those messier everyday moments, whether they involve a team member getting sick, a kid melting down, or realizing that we have too much on our plate. How we respond when the overwhelm bubbles up makes all the difference. How do you typically respond when you're feeling overwhelmed? These are the most common answers I hear:

- Push harder, work longer, and beat yourself up for not doing more
- Procrastinate by starting then stopping to check social media or do anything except the important thing you need to do
- Become almost paralyzed and have trouble focusing because of the stress of all the other things you have to do
- Break out in tears or become impatient with the people you love
- Tell yourself that you'll take a break when you get all caught up
- Lose focus and take much longer to complete a task
- Shut down and feel unable to do anything.

Do any of these sound familiar? What does your overwhelm look like? Remember, there's nothing wrong with you! But you need to understand that when you're overwhelmed, you're *less* focused and productive. As Tim Ferriss says, "Being overwhelmed is often as unproductive as doing nothing, and is far more unpleasant."

Unexpected things will happen. Things rarely go exactly as planned. You'll sometimes take on too much even when you're great at prioritizing. You're going to have to make choices and adjust. And when you slow it down and choose to remain calm, you can shift from being overwhelmed day after day—living in a state of chronic overwhelm—to being overwhelmed for maybe fifteen minutes or an hour or an afternoon at the most.

Calmness isn't just the lack of being overwhelmed, but a way of being. You can learn how to navigate the unexpected or stressful situations with more calm, presence, and ease. You don't have to let the overwhelm take over. And when it does, you can remind yourself that you have a choice how you respond.

That said, it's likely you do have too many things to do right now, especially if you haven't YET started setting boundaries, prioritizing your time, focusing on the right things, and saying no to a whole lot more.

You've already learned about ways of thinking and actions that can help you feel less overwhelmed. In this chapter, I'm going to share some different ways to think about overwhelm and some more tools to help you step out of it. I'll also reinforce some key points.

STEP OUT OF THE CONSTANT, DAILY OVERWHELM

What do you do when you're so far in and feel as if the crushing workload is impossible to get out of because you've already committed to everything? How can you get back on track and still deliver results when you're feeling overwhelmed?

One of the biggest mistakes people make when they're overwhelmed is the one I used to make—they try to work even harder, which leaves them feeling even more overwhelmed and burned out.

I get it. You have a lot to do. Just ask anyone how they're doing and you'll likely hear, "I have so much to do!" (And they're secretly super overwhelmed but don't tell you that part.) You might still find yourself saying this and buying into the belief that doing more means you're being more productive, which will lead to accomplishing more and, therefore, being more successful. It's almost as if you feel lazy and unproductive if you aren't doing something. Don't be mistaken—it's a trap!

With this approach of constant overwhelm, it's taking you more effort to get the same or a lesser result. This is the paradox of overwhelm. Too much to do equals little progress on anything. The time that you spend worrying about getting a task done, panicking about what will happen if you don't—this is time spent not getting done the very thing you need to get done! Plus, the overwhelm is costing you other things, such as enjoying your work and personal time, feeling good, or having strong relationships with the people you care about.

Think about it. Does everyone who's really overwhelmed reach their goals more quickly? Are they showing up as their best selves? And even if they look successful, what's it costing them? Their health, quality of life, patience, relationships with their family? When you take on more and do more, do you feel as if you're moving faster toward your goals, or do you feel less in control? It's likely the latter. It's time to let go of the belief that you need to work harder and do more, especially when you're overwhelmed.

It's not that you "can't handle it." It's too much in the first place! Or maybe you do have a reasonable workload, but your attention is focused on everything you need to do (which is inherently overwhelming) rather than on one thing at a time.

Getting things done without doing more

Overwhelm often stems from having too many "priorities" or a mile-long to-do list. When you have less to manage, you can accomplish more of what really matters. You're also more productive, focused, and present. Mindfulness can help you recognize when you're feeling overwhelm and the root cause of it—in this case, too much to do. With this awareness, you can make better choices, such as saying no to something or focusing your attention on one thing at a time. Or perhaps, if you've been working a long stretch or feeling too overwhelmed, it's time for a break to reset.

I've found there are two steps to approaching overwhelm. First, you must say 'no' more and take things off your plate to avoid becoming overcommitted. This is where honouring your values, boundaries, and priorities is essential (you've already identified these things—time to put this into practice!). Focus on what's important and let go of what isn't. Doing less will help you step out of the daily overwhelm. It really is OKAY!

Second, you need to master calming your mind and listening to what you need when you're overwhelmed in the moment.

STEP OUT OF OVERWHELMING MOMENTS

Do you ever find that one minute you feel on top of everything and the next you feel overwhelmed with it all? It can sometimes be tricky to know whether you actually have too much on your plate and need to prioritize better or if you're letting distractions and overwhelm take over unnecessarily in the moment—and just need to focus or take a breather to reset.

I still sometimes walk that fine line of wondering whether I have too much on the go or I'm just letting the pressure I put on myself get to me.

When the pressure of the tasks ahead bears down. When you feel the weight of the expectations. When you start to doubt that you can deliver. These are the moments when, instead of pushing yourself to do more (and more), it's better to pause. To step out of the overwhelm and get perspective so you know what action to take.

When you're overwhelmed, you're *not* present.

So what can you do in the moments when the overwhelm bubbles up?

Start by acknowledging how you're feeling, without judgment! Then ask yourself one (or more) of these questions.

- **What matters most right now?** Focus on THIS and limit all other distractions. Instead of thinking about the hundred things you have to do, focus on the one thing that needs your attention most right now.

- **What do I really need right now?** Maybe taking a break or going for a walk or talking to someone will be just what you need to move forward. Remember, feeling overwhelmed is just as unproductive as doing nothing, so give yourself permission to focus on your needs. This may seem counterintuitive, but listening to what you need will help you calm your mind and step out of the overwhelm.

- **What do I need to care about less or take off my plate?** Get closer to the heart of what really matters and let go of what doesn't.

Ask yourself these questions daily and practice navigating the overwhelming moments with more ease.

When it comes to stepping out of the overwhelm, pay attention to what works (and what doesn't work) for you, as everyone is different. Here are some other strategies and tools you might want to try. Some we've already talked about but important to reinforce.

Reduce stress in the "pressure-cooker" moments. I call those habitual stressful times in your day or week—the ones where you're regularly misaligned with your values or overwhelmed and stressed out—the pressure-cooker moments. Maybe your pressure-cooker moment is Sunday afternoons, when you feel anxiety about the upcoming week (the "Sunday scaries"). Maybe it's when you leave the house in the morning, when you're rushing out the door to get to work on time, or maybe it's the thirty minutes after work when you're rushing through supper to get to a kid's activity.

Create buffers around the times that you know are going to be stressful and actively look at what you can do to handle the situation better and more calmly. For example, if I went back to my corporate career, I'd set a boundary: no 8:00 a.m. meetings. If I had to attend a meeting (say I didn't have control over the timing and it was required), I would give myself more buffer at home in the mornings. This would reduce the stress around getting out the door in the morning.

Reducing stress in a pressure-cooker moment might mean saying no to spending time with someone who drains your energy, or blocking off Monday mornings so you can let go of stressing out on Sunday afternoons, or leaving work ten minutes early. What are the pressure-cooker moments for you? What boundaries can you put in place to make those everyday moments less stressful and set yourself up for success?

Break things down and keep it simple. It's amazing how much you can cut out when you strive for simplicity instead of perfection. And when you look at the great big list or project, it's easy to feel overwhelmed. Break down what you need to do into smaller chunks to focus on. For example, instead of focusing on the big, important report you need to write, focus on getting the outline done. Then focus on the next thing. And the next thing. You'll move through your work more quickly and feel a greater sense of control.

Tight for time? Ask yourself, *What's the simplest way to accomplish the outcome I want in the time I do have?* Or, *If I could get only one thing done in the next hour, what would it be?*

Take a breather and figure out your next right move. Again, it can be really tempting to keep going, going, going, but slowing down is essential. This breather time will help you notice how your thoughts and actions are helping you or hindering you and will help you think more clearly so you can focus on the right things. It might look like taking an afternoon off to reset. Or taking fifteen minutes to go for a walk or to start your day strategically prioritizing. These things will make a huge difference in your ability to refocus on what's important.

The old me, when feeling overwhelmed, would hunker down, stay in that stressful state, and skip my evening or weekend plans. Now I listen to what I need and go where that leads me.

Don't fall into the trap of being a victim. Avoid a victim mentality when you're overwhelmed. When you're in this place, it's common to feel paralyzed by stress and demands, which leads to a downward spiral of thinking there's nothing you can do and continuing to take on more and more (so you become more overwhelmed). Remember, you have a choice. Adjust your expectations and perspective, say no to something, and seek solutions to improve it. I used to fall into the victim trap daily. These days it might happen once every few months, when the overwhelm gets too high. We can get back in the driver's seat and take ownership of our time and situation.

Stick to your boundaries around your time—they're there for a reason! The line between work and personal life can often be blurred, leading to a constant state of being "on"—and a constant sense of overwhelm. Strong boundaries, particularly around work hours, are among the most effective antidotes.

Leaving work on time isn't just a logistical act; it shows your commitment to your well-being and work-life balance. It draws a clear line between professional responsibilities and personal time, and this allows your mind and body to recharge and engage fully with life outside of work. This separation is crucial, as it helps prevent work overwhelm from seeping into your personal life and helps you to be more focused when you are at work.

Even if you love your job, it's important to take time away from the office and to create and maintain space in your calendar during the workday. These acts of self-care pay dividends in mental clarity—which means less overwhelm! Remember, white space isn't about doing nothing. Unscheduled blocks of time offer you an opportunity to breathe, reflect, and reset when you need it, which is a critical step toward balanced days.

Accept that you'll never have enough time for it all. This kind of acceptance is freeing. Instead of wasting your mental energy on worrying about not having enough time, accept that you don't and move your attention to what really matters. Remember, there will always be more to do.

While I sometimes still feel "behind" or think *I don't have enough time for it all!* these feelings and thoughts don't have the same power over me that they used to. I've also noticed that regardless of whether I have a full workweek or I'm at the lake on vacation, that voice creeps up: *I don't have enough time.* This leads me to remember that I won't ever have time for it all.

Acknowledging this can instantly relieve the feeling of being overwhelmed. Don't waste mental energy on that same old story. Move on.

Focus on the wins. So often we put tremendous unnecessary pressure on ourselves (especially women) and end up carrying a constant feeling of not doing enough. Shoulda, woulda, coulda. Cut yourself some slack and give yourself credit for what you're doing and how you're showing up. Be kinder to yourself. Let go of the feeling of not doing enough and you'll feel more peaceful (even if you have to let go one hundred times a day).

Don't underestimate the power of a simple action such as writing out three wins every day, or to at least take a minute and make a mental note of them. What did you do to contribute or show up in the way that you wanted to? What lesson did you learn from something that didn't go well? What small step forward did you take?

It's too easy to focus on everything you didn't do—put the focus on what you did do! When you give yourself permission to acknowledge that today you gave your best and tomorrow is a new day, life gets a little easier to navigate.

Take something off your plate. Remember, it's okay to say no. I've said it already, and this is an obvious one, but it bears repeating. When you take that breather, ask yourself, *What needs to come off my plate?* Delegate it, delay it, or just put it on hold indefinitely. Sometimes you'll even need to put on hold what's important, so you can give it the attention it deserves. Go back to your list of things you could say no to and give yourself permission to actually say no. Your future self will thank you. Your current self probably will too, as you'll likely feel a weight lift from your shoulders immediately.

Ask for help. This is about more than delegating. It's about being okay with saying "I could use some help here" and letting others handle things too (you don't need to be the one taking it all on—this can lead to burnout). Others might offer different perspectives on or solutions to the problems you're facing. They might suggest approaches or ideas that you hadn't considered— ones that are more effective.

Talk to someone about how you're feeling. Acknowledging that you're overwhelmed and then reaching out for assistance can significantly reduce stress and anxiety levels. It's a proactive step toward managing your overwhelm and ensuring that you can continue to perform effectively.

Shift your perspective. When you're feeling overwhelmed, pay attention to what story you're telling yourself and look at your situation from a different perspective. For example, shift, *There's no way I'm going to get everything done* to *I'm helping my team to be successful* or, *In the end, it always works out* or, *I have time for what matters.* And try to acknowledge unhelpful thoughts with kindness. Say "Let it go" out loud (yes it can feel silly, but it works) and reframe: *What's a better way to see the situation? What matters most right now? What are the wins?*

I tell myself, *I show up for what matters most.* This helps me feel better about dropping what's less important! On the days I feel more behind, I will focus even more on the wins.

Choose to remain calm. This is where mindfulness can really serve you. Remember, it's a choice. You are where your attention is—so the more you focus on feeling overwhelmed, the more overwhelmed you'll feel. The more you practice being present or meditate or build your mindfulness muscle in another way, the easier it is to remain calm throughout your day. When you're overwhelmed, you lose perspective, get stuck in paralysis, and forget you're in control. And things end up being *way* harder than they need to be. When you're calm, you think more clearly and make better choices. You're more present and navigate stressful moments with more ease. You get to choose.

Give yourself permission to slow down and do less. When you find yourself in that overwhelmed state, your instinct will likely be to keep on going. You might want to cancel family time or exercise plans to work late, which will hurt your happiness and performance in the long run. Remember that when you're in this overwhelmed state, you're not getting done what needs to be done.

It's far more productive to step back and identify what you need to feel better.

Take a walk or a coffee break, do something kind for someone, listen to a favourite song, or carve out focus time for deep work—whatever helps to get you back into a clearer headspace, so you can figure out the action that will move you forward.

Ask yourself those questions: *What matters most right now? What do I really need right now? What do I care about less right now?* The words "right now" bring you back to the present moment and figure out your next step.

Most importantly, be okay with doing what works for YOU. What works for one individual might not be as effective for another. It might also be different for you depending on the day. You don't need to try *all* the strategies (that might be overwhelming in itself). Instead, pay attention to what helps you. Ask yourself: what do I really need? With some reflection and awareness of your stressors, you'll uncover what helps you to step out of the overwhelm.

Self-Awareness and Action:
WHAT HELPS YOU FEEL LESS OVERWHELMED?

Take some time to identify clear actions that can help you step out of the overwhelm. Reflect on these questions and write out freely whatever comes up for you.

- What does overwhelm look like for you? Is it a constant state or moments in your day? How do you show up when you're feeling overwhelmed?

- What are your pressure-cooker moments? What can you do to relieve some of the pressure or handle those stressful situations with more calm and ease?

- Where can you take something off your plate or extend a deadline to give yourself some breathing space? Let it go. You will instantly feel lighter. What can you start saying no to more to avoid overcommitting in the first place?

- What helps you when you're feeling overwhelmed? Write out five to ten small things that help you feel calm and better. Do at least one of these things the next time you feel overwhelmed.

- What new mindset could you adopt or story could you tell yourself when you feel overwhelmed? What question will you ask yourself when you feel overwhelmed?

Be bold. What is one thing you can do today that will help you feel less overwhelmed? Give yourself permission to do that!

We often feel overwhelmed because we worry about meeting others' expectations or achieving perfection, leading to guilt when we fall short. This magnifies our stress and steers us in a direction that isn't right for us. This is what we'll dive into next.

Chapter 9

TURN DOWN THE VOLUME ON WORRY AND GUILT

"You wouldn't worry so much about what others think of you if you realized how seldom they do."

– Eleanor Roosevelt

My dog got sick with only a few days left in my corporate career. My little Yorkie, Tazer, had been my best friend for years. He was there through a divorce in my mid-twenties, my forever marriage, having kids, fun times and challenging times. I loved that dog dearly. But the older Tazer got and the busier my husband and I got with the kids, the more he sometimes felt like an annoyance (it makes me sad to type this, as it reminds me of how misaligned I was).

When Tazer got suddenly sick, I knew something was unusually wrong but didn't know how bad it was. My instinct said, *Stay home and take care of him today.* But the louder voice in my head told me to go to the office. Even though I was leaving my job because I wanted to be more present and focus on what really mattered to me and not miss out on my life.

I need to go to the office, I told myself. *I have too much to do. What would people think if I took a day off now?* And so I went to work that day (and so did my husband) and the dog spent the day alone. I prioritized my work because I was worried about what people would think, even though I know that my co-workers would have been great. I was the one putting that pressure on myself.

And when we got home from work that day, Tazer was so much sicker. My husband and I took him to the vet that evening and were told that he'd have to be put to sleep. The vet didn't say whether if we had brought him in sooner, we could have done something to save him—by the sounds of it, it would have happened regardless (or maybe the vet was just saying that to ease our guilt).

I'd like to think that had I known it was the last day with Tazer, I would have stayed home. But I didn't. I went to work, even though what I really wanted was to be with my dog, to cuddle and comfort him. It likely wouldn't have changed the outcome, but I could have spent that last day with him. It was a choice within my control, but I didn't choose wisely. I'd been too wrapped up in worry about what people would think. I didn't yet have the presence or confidence to ignore everything else and focus on what mattered most that day.

This is one of a small number of regrets I have. The story brings me to tears as I write it. I can remember that feeling of heartache and guilt. At that point in my life, I'm not sure anything had ever hurt as much as putting him to sleep. I'd like to go back and change how I handled that day and the choice I made. I wasn't present for that moment that mattered because I was more focused on and worried about my work, even though everything at work would have been fine if I hadn't gone in that day.

I was leaving my job so I wouldn't miss out on my life, and life was happening right there in that moment. I wasn't focusing on what really mattered. My worry and guilt were in the wrong place.

THE MESSY LESSON AND KEY SHIFT

That day taught me to not let worry about my to-do list or what other people might think keep me from something that's more important in the moment. I wasn't yet living with the intention to focus on what matters most every day. I could have figured out the work situation later. I could have made up the time, if necessary. I used to waste a lot of my mental energy on worry and guilt, and it drove a lot of my decisions.

Worry and guilt steal our attention from the present moment and what really matters, waste our time and energy, and block actions and decisions that are right for us.

Of course, we can't control every moment. We might miss something important. That's life too. The point is to listen to your instincts more. I knew deep down it was more important for me to stay home that day. I didn't, though. I didn't have confidence in my choices. Don't let worry and guilt lead you in the wrong direction.

Another important lesson I learned that day, and one that I live every day now, is to **be present for the moments that matter**. Because you won't get them back. The big and small ones. Moments with your kids, with a friend who's struggling, with your pet, with yourself.

This lesson would come to serve me in a much bigger way than I ever could have imagined, which I'll tell you about in Chapter 12.

Take the time when the moment calls for it. You never know what tomorrow will bring. This is why it's so important to be present. To make mindful choices that reflect who you want to be and how you want to show up.

A big part of my decision to go to work that day and not stay home with Tazer was because I let the worry and guilt cloud my thinking and stop me from taking action that was aligned with my values.

WORRY AND GUILT ARE THE REAL PROBLEM

I used to spend A LOT of time worrying about what other people thought of me and feeling guilty about letting people down, especially when I was exhausted and spread thin. I'd replay every little detail of a conversation that hadn't gone well. I'd feel guilty whenever I said no.

What if I don't get a task done by the deadline? What if I said something wrong in the meeting? What if someone thinks less of me now because I said no to them?

We worry about what we're doing "wrong" or how things will go and then feel guilty about whatever we chose to do. Yet this creates an even BIGGER issue.

That's the real problem—the worry or guilt. Not whatever you're worrying or feeling guilty **about**.

Again, they are often huge wastes of our time and mental energy. They lead to higher anxiety, undercut our performance, and don't feel very good. They block purposeful action and keep you from doing what you deep down want to do. Most importantly, they keep you out of the present moment and missing what's going on right in front of you.

Worry and guilt are interconnected in the way that they affect our sense of balance, well-being, and performance. In certain contexts, these emotional states are helpful—guilt and worry can reflect what we care about and help guide our choices when in the right place. But most of the time, they're the problem in themselves.

Worry tends to be unpleasant thoughts and ruminating about a situation with an uncertain outcome, such as:

- Advancing in your career and achieving your professional goals
- Not having enough time to meet all your work deadlines
- The perceived pressure to perform perfectly in every role
- Maintaining good health, managing stress, and finding time for exercise
- What other people think of you and your choices
- What happened in the past or what might happen in the future
- Being a good parent (for example, worrying about whether you're spending quality time with your kids or making the right decisions regarding their upbringing).

Guilt is a feeling of remorse or regret about something you did or failed to do. It arises when you believe you caused harm to someone or did something wrong, such as:

- Making a mistake, especially if it affects others
- Not keeping a commitment or breaking a promise to someone
- Taking time for yourself, especially if you perceive it as being at the expense of others' needs or expectations
- Feeling bad about not returning calls or messages
- Prioritizing work responsibilities over spending time with family or friends
- Missing a deadline or being late for a meeting
- Saying no to a request or being unable to help someone.

We worry excessively about unlikely events or feel guilty about actions that, on reflection, weren't that big of a deal.

Similarly, worry and guilt can often be misplaced—as in, not aligned with what really matters to you and instead aligned with the opinions of people whose opinions don't truly matter. When I stopped overworking, I had to give myself a pep talk about "turning down the volume" every day, telling myself it didn't matter what that VP or that colleague thought of me—what mattered was what my family thought of me.

You might argue, "If I don't worry or feel guilty, my problems don't just go away." But how much time are you spending on the worry or guilt instead of focusing your attention on what you want or how to make the situation better? I used to think that worrying was part of problem-solving, not realizing that all that worry (and guilt) used a tremendous amount of mental energy. As a result, I was blocking myself from taking action and creating more undesired outcomes.

When you're worrying or feeling guilty about something, your flashlight is often shining in an unhelpful direction. Your attention is focused on what could or did go wrong, thereby increasing the chances that things will go wrong.

The more you focus your attention on the worry and guilt, the more you'll worry and feel guilty.

When you worry or feel guilty about something, do you feel as if doing so is helping you accomplish your goals faster? Are you moving forward in a positive and productive way? Are you making choices aligned with your values, boundaries, and priorities?

It's more likely that you aren't taking the action you know you need to take, so you keep spiraling, constantly worrying or feeling guilty about something when, in fact... it's the worry or guilt that's your real problem.

As mentioned, though, sometimes worry and guilt can serve a purpose. They can be cues to pay attention to something you care about.

HELPFUL UNEASE

Worry and guilt, when channeled constructively, can be valuable tools.

Let's start with guilt, which comes from the feeling that you're doing something wrong. The thing is, in many cases there is no true right or wrong—it's about what's important to you and feels right for you. If you're making choices that are NOT aligned with your values or what really matters to you or who you want to be, guilt can benefit you. It can direct you to the real issue.

Without being hard on yourself, ask, *What is this guilt trying to tell me?*

For example, if I yell at my kids and then feel guilty about it, the guilt is understandable because this isn't the parent I want to be. Or when I chose not to take the day with my dog, that guilt I felt about not being there was telling me that my decision wasn't aligned with my values.

The trick is to notice the guilt, check in with what it's telling you, and then take action to make it better or learn from it and let it go. Continuing to hold on to the guilt just wastes your energy and keeps you in the unhelpful habit of being hard on yourself.

Now let's look at how worry can be helpful. Worry serves as a natural protective mechanism, signaling that something important to us is at stake. It keeps us alert, ensuring that we're paying close attention. Healthy worry—that is, heightened awareness—about our relationships, work responsibilities, or well-being, for example, can lead to more thoughtful decisions and actions regarding these things and, in turn, better outcomes. However, worry becomes counterproductive when it becomes an overwhelming presence or when it's about situations that are out of our control.

Negative emotions are a cue to pay attention and can help us. Anxiety can be a reminder to prepare for important events or challenges. Guilt can serve as a moral compass, indicating where actions are not aligned with what is truly important to you. Overwhelm can let you know that you have too much on the go or that you're putting too much pressure on yourself. These emotions, while often uncomfortable, can prompt introspection, growth, and adaptability. Understanding and respecting them rather than labelling them as "bad" is part of healthy self-awareness.

But what often happens—and is one-hundred-percent NOT helpful—is that we feel guilty and worry about choices that ARE aligned with what we value or want or need. Or it's excessive. For example, maybe you say no to a new project at work because you're already spread thin or want to focus on a priority but then feel guilty and worry about what your manager thinks of you. Or you decline an invite to a family get-together because you need some personal time or don't want to go but then feel guilty and worry about what your family will think.

This kind of guilt and worry steals your presence. It steals your joy. It leaves you feeling more stressed out and less balanced. It wastes your time and energy. And you miss out on enjoying the benefit of doing the thing you really want to do!

BUT WHAT WILL PEOPLE THINK OF ME?

When you reduce the amount of time and energy spent on worrying or feeling guilty, you open up more opportunities to see solutions, feel less stressed and enjoy life and its everyday moments more. I understand why you might worry about what people will think or what might happen, or why you might feel guilty about your choices. But as long as you keep giving in to worry and guilt, you'll continue wasting your precious time and energy and letting it hold you back from taking action on what you want.

When I decided to stop working evenings and weekends during the most demanding time in my corporate career, my biggest fear was *What will people think of me?* Before going into every meeting for which I hadn't spent my usual extra hours making everything perfect (didn't have time for that), I had to remind myself, *It doesn't matter what they think of me.* Whenever I chose not to take my laptop home and had to say no to someone . . . *It doesn't matter what they think of me.* I had to repeatedly remind myself of this in order to have the courage to stick to my boundaries.

This doesn't mean I didn't care. I still cared about showing up and giving my best and doing a great job. It was that I stopped letting others' opinions define me. I had to choose to care more about what I wanted and my values, and to care more about the opinions of those who mattered most to me, like my husband and kids. I had to choose to be the parent I wanted to be, which meant being present in the evenings and on vacation. I had to choose to be the leader I wanted to be for my team, which meant not asking them to sacrifice their personal time.

Worrying about what other people think of you or feeling guilty based on others' opinions are common experiences that can significantly influence your actions and mental well-being.

Another common area that gets our worry is ruminating on the worst-case scenarios. *What if they think I'm not pulling my weight? What if I fail? What if things don't get better or this goes terribly? What if they don't like me anymore?*

This catastrophic thinking leads us to overestimate the threat and **underestimate our ability to cope.** When we slip into worrying about all the things that can go wrong (thereby devaluing ourselves or what could go right), both our happiness and performance are undercut. This tends to happen when there's ambiguity, something you value is at stake, you fear the situation, or you're already run-down and depleted.

We can also get caught up in unhelpful worries and guilt when we assume we know what other people are thinking (this is my biggest nemesis), blame others, take things personally, think we have no choice, or ruminate on what happened in the past (you literally cannot change what happened in the past).

What people often don't understand is that their worry and guilt are what get in the way of them performing at their best and living a life they want. They hold back. They don't say what needs to be said. They don't ask for what they need. Or they do and then waste their energy on worry and guilt afterward. What other people think and do is also outside of your control.

If this resonates with you, it's time to turn down the volume. You'll be more present, feel more confident, and make better choices that are a reflection of your values and what you want.

TURN DOWN THE VOLUME

By turning down the volume, I mean reducing the intensity and impact of worry and guilt. It doesn't mean completely eliminating these emotions, which are natural. It's about being mindful and managing them so that they don't overwhelm or dominate your thoughts and hold you back. You can quiet them to the point where they don't block action or leave you feeling bad about yourself. You can move your attention—shine your flashlight—in a direction that serves you better. You can welcome more balance and presence into your life.

Though I feel as if I've mastered the art of keeping boundaries and saying no, thoughts such as *What will people think?* or *Am I getting it wrong?* still pop up daily. Thankfully, I've learned how to calm my mind and turn down the volume. I'm not sure you can get rid of all the worry and guilt—unless you're a Zen leader, perhaps, or my husband—but you can feel these emotions less and be present more. Kenton and I have learned to balance each other out!

The awesome news is that worrying and feeling guilty are habits. And you can always create new habits. I was once a chronic worrier so, if I can worry less, so can you! Here's what helped me learn to turn down the volume on worry and guilt. I still practice the following today. We touched on some of these in the chapter on being present, not perfect.

First, notice your thoughts and where your attention is. Whenever you're feeling worried or guilty, you're not in the present moment. The trick is to catch yourself—to notice when you're distracted, caught up in worry and guilt. Noticing where your attention is allows you to return to the present and redirect your focus.

Don't be hard on yourself; simply be aware and observe. Where is your attention? What unhelpful thoughts are you having? What is the guilt telling you? Noticing, without judgment, is often enough to turn the volume down.

Practicing mindfulness helps you move your focus to the present moment, reducing worries about the future or guilt about the past. Meditation can also help you understand and manage these emotions.

Focus on what you're saying yes to. This is my favourite. Remind yourself why you're making a certain choice. Why is saying no to this particular thing important to you? What are you saying yes to instead? How are you showing up for what matters more? Getting clear on this can drown out the guilt and worry.

My clients make the biggest gains in letting go of guilt once they get clear on what matters more and focus on that. It's more empowering than feeling bad about yourself or worrying about what others will think for making a choice that's right for you.

Become more aware of your unhelpful thoughts. We tend to worry about the *same* things and feel guilty about the *same* things—day after day! We all have unhelpful thoughts and patterns, but again, when you notice, you can make a new choice. It's not about never worrying and feeling guilty again. It's about catching yourself, over and over. Whether it's catastrophic thinking, taking things personally, or assuming you know what someone else is thinking.

The more you become aware of your unhelpful thoughts and patterns, the easier it becomes to notice when you fall into them and then move your attention.

Challenge and reframe your thoughts. Once you notice an unhelpful thought, you can choose a thought or perspective that serves you better. Your perspective is subjective. Remember, our minds can make things seem small and manageable or big and daunting. Challenge and reframe your thoughts with questions such as these:

- What's a better way to see the situation?
- When you find yourself worrying about all the things that could go wrong, consider: *What's the worst thing that could happen? What's the best thing that could happen? What's most likely to happen?* Put your attention on a positive outcome.
- What *can* you do? (Focus on this instead of what you can't do.)

Consider whether the worry or guilt is helping you to move forward in a positive and productive way or is just amplifying all the worst-case scenarios. And consider whether you're taking action on things within your control and focusing on what really matters.

Don't pile on the negative thoughts and emotions. It's normal for worries and guilt to pop up. But what often happens next just makes everything worse—you pile on the negative thoughts and emotions. You feel bad about feeling guilty. Or you're hard on yourself because you're worrying about what someone thinks. The piling on doesn't help you, so let it go! Let's just agree now to stop doing that.

Beating yourself up about what you did or didn't do doesn't help anyone, especially not you. Self-compassion is key.

Let your own values, needs, and wants guide you. Don't let your self-worth be tied up in what other people think of you. We can use other people or their opinions as benchmarks for determining our value as a person. Let your inner world—your values, needs, strengths, etc.—be the compass that guides your decisions rather than letting the outside world—what everyone else thinks—dictate how you think and what actions you take.

This will also help you focus on what you're saying yes to instead of what you're saying no to, and you'll feel more confident in your choices.

Let. It. Go. As the *Frozen* song says, *Let It Go!* The truth is, people will judge you. Things won't always go the way you want. Someone might not like what you choose to do. You'll make mistakes—it's human nature. If it's outside of your control, let it go! You won't please everyone, regardless of what you do. Once you accept this, it gets easier to turn down the volume and take action. Let go of the worry and guilt and come back to the present.

Ask yourself, "If I weren't worried about what people might think, what would I do?" This question can help you instantly get to the heart of what you really want to do and figure out what choice is aligned with that. When you let go of the worry about what people might think, you can instantly gain confidence.

Finally, when you're worrying or feeling guilty, try visualizing turning down the volume with a dial.

Everything you learned in Chapter 7 about being present and building the mindfulness muscle will serve you when it comes to quieting your worry and guilt as well. It will help you make room for more presence, more joy, and more time and energy for what you want.

Also remember the importance of the basics. Eat well, move your body, and sleep—all these things contribute to a healthier mind. It's WAY easier to fall into overwhelm, worry, and guilt when you're exhausted and run down, so take the time you need to rest and recharge. Listen to what your mind and body are telling you.

Worry and guilt still find their way into my days. I worry about how my kids are doing and whether I'm hitting the mark in a presentation or what someone will think of me for saying no. Yet, the worries and guilt that once seemed overwhelming are now met with quiet acceptance and turning down the volume. The journey isn't about silencing worry and guilt entirely but about learning to quiet them. It's a habit. And you can create a new habit.

Self-Awareness and Action:
HOW WILL YOU TURN DOWN THE VOLUME?

Take some time to practice being more mindful—try to catch yourself when you're worrying or feeling guilty so you can turn down the volume. Reflect on these questions and write out freely whatever comes up for you.

- What's something you've been holding back from out of fear of being judged? If you weren't worried about what people might think, what would you do?

- Think about a stressful situation. If you stripped away the worry and guilt involved in it, how would you feel? What action would you take? How would you show up differently?

- Think of a challenging situation involving something that really matters to you. What are the unhelpful thoughts that come up? For each of these unhelpful thoughts, write down a thought that's more helpful and something you could do instead of dwelling on the unhelpful thought.

- What is something you're feeling guilty about but know is the right choice for you? What are you saying yes to instead? (Focus on this.)

- What question or phrase might help you turn down the volume the next time the worry or guilt pops up? Give yourself a mantra or way of reframing your thoughts so you can put your energy into taking purposeful action instead.

Be bold. If you weren't worried about what other people might think, what's one thing you would do this week? Go do that.

It gets easier to balance your life and make choices aligned for you as you manage your worry and guilt better. When you let go of worrying about what other people think, you'll also instantly gain confidence. This is what we'll explore next.

Chapter 10

FEEL CONFIDENT IN YOURSELF AND YOUR CHOICES

"Success is liking yourself, liking what you do and liking how you do it."

– Maya Angelou

My only plan when I left my corporate career was to figure out a plan. I had no idea what I'd do, but I knew I needed a little space to figure it out. So I took four months off to enjoy the rest of the summer and reflect on what was next for me.

I eventually decided to start my own business, which would involve coaching, workshops and speaking, and writing. I was fascinated with the question: How can we be our best *with* all the demands and expectations? I wanted to help other leaders (at all levels) struggling with some of the same things I'd been struggling with—those who also wanted to be more balanced in life and their best selves at work and at home.

I had never aspired to be an entrepreneur, yet it felt like the next right move. I believed it would give me the flexibility and fulfillment I was seeking, as well as set me up to enjoy and be more present in my life. I could work from home, design my business around the hours I wanted to work and the lifestyle my family and I desired, and have a bigger impact. I confidently and even naively thought that this would be an easier path (easier than my corporate career, at least).

To my surprise, it wasn't so easy. It was exciting to create my own thing, but it also meant wearing *all* the hats. There was no longer an IT department to call. I was IT . . . and Finance and Marketing and HR! It took longer to see the results I wanted. And, while I had supportive people in my life, there were also a lot of voices telling me that the way I wanted to run my business wouldn't work.

So many people, from marketing coaches to other business owners to friends of friends, told me I'd need to hustle, work really hard, and sacrifice my personal time if I wanted to be "successful." An instructor in my coaching certification program said, "You must sacrifice your family time for at least two years to get your business up and running, so get your husband to take the kids to their activities, stop volunteering, and focus as much of your time and energy on your business as you can."

I had another coach bluntly say to me, "It's nonsense that you want to help other people be more balanced. It will never work—it's impossible." The word *impossible* only fueled me more. *Let me show you!* I thought. (They weren't a very good coach).

At one point, I was working with a business coach in the U.S. whose big in-person event for their clients was on the Canada Day long weekend. I decided not to go, even though I was paying a lot of money for the program. July long weekend was my favourite time of the year. It was the weekend we kicked off summer, and family and friend time. I didn't want to go on the trip and my absence at the lake that weekend would've been very noticeable. If the event had been on another weekend that summer, perhaps. But not that one. When I told my coach I wasn't going, he said, "If you don't make your business number one, you'll never succeed."

Well, I thought, *my business will never be number one. So I'm going to have to figure out a different way to succeed.*

I was surprised by just how many people told me I'd need to hustle and give up my family and personal time. I remember often thinking, *I'd JUST learned this lesson in my corporate career!* Here I was, starting my own business to gain freedom and flexibility, yet the messages and expectations were quite different. The elusive "if you just work hard enough and long enough, THEN you will be successful and can have the life you want" belief seemed to be everywhere.

But I was not willing to sacrifice what really mattered to me and I was committed to creating success on my terms, even though people were telling me I had to do it a different way. So, from day one, I've been very intentional about building and growing my business in a way that offers me the balance I want in my life.

I had this invisible line that I wasn't willing to cross. I wasn't willing to compromise my values or personal time or burn myself out to hit a goal.

Now, I highly value personal development and learning from others, and I wouldn't be where I am today without all I learned from those same coaches and programs and mentors. Working with them, my confidence grew as I became more competent in running a business.

With any advice or guidance from others, we need to discern what our intuition tells us and what's helpful. And to be okay ignoring what isn't right for us. (Even with this book, I want you to choose and act on what's right for *you*).

To this day, I consider what success looks like to me within this context: *How do I want to live and show up in my life? What would it look like to be balanced and have a thriving business? How can I lead by example and walk my talk?* This is the game that I'm playing.

You're now playing a different game too!

Making choices that are right for you—and what success looks like in your life—takes a deeper inner confidence and trust in yourself. That you'll be okay and you can figure it out.

This all said, even though I was firm in my conviction to remain balanced as I grew my business, I also doubted myself A LOT. Every time someone told me to hustle, or that I'd never be successful if I kept building my business in the way I was, or that my goals weren't big enough, or that I wasn't doing enough, or when I didn't take someone's advice, I'd doubt myself. I'd overthink it. I'd slow down my momentum. I'd worry. *What if I get it wrong?* Other people's opinions chipped away at my confidence and belief in myself.

The doubts and fears still get in my head (this is probably the biggest area I work on myself these days). I've just learned to turn down the volume and feel more confident in myself and my choices.

You can too!

THE MESSY LESSON AND KEY SHIFT

Starting my own business taught me that there will always be people who will tell us what we should or shouldn't do. The thing is that success looks different to everyone. And that's okay! We can all do life the way we want. I'm not here to judge anyone else's choices—I'm here to make my own choices. We also have to be aware that our doubts and fears can slow our momentum or keep us from taking actions aligned with what really matters to us.

This is why it's so important to get clear on what success looks and feels like to you—not what it looks like for others or society or what you see on social media. When we know what we stand for (and what we don't) and our priorities, we're more likely to speak up in a meeting or say no to someone. On the flip side, the more you identify with what others think of you or your busy badge, the more value you attach to these things and the harder it can be to take action that aligns with the balanced life and leader you want to be.

By becoming more in tune with what we value, choices that are right for us, and how we think about ourselves, we can take more purposeful action in the outside world.

We can express choices that correspond with our values, needs, priorities, strengths, beliefs, etc. "Here I am and this is how I do it." We can feel more confident in ourselves, no matter our role or experience.

Learning to trust in yourself and let your choices come from within is key not only to creating more balance in your life but also to feeling balanced within yourself. Plus, you waste a lot of time and mental energy doubting and overthinking your every move (ask me how I know).

Fear and doubts are also normal, especially when you're doing something new, important, or uncomfortable. But understand that your fears and doubts—as well as your confidence—are products of your mind. And as you've learned, you have more control over your thoughts and beliefs than you might realize.

CONFIDENCE ON DEMAND

Many people think confidence is something you either have or you don't. But what I've noticed and experienced is that you can tap into confidence on demand. Yes, confidence grows the more you take action and develop competence. But how you think about yourself in any given moment can also lead you to feel confident—or to seriously doubt yourself. So I see confidence as a big mind game.

It's more rooted in the stories we tell ourselves and the self-talk we engage in daily.

Ever experience where you feel confident when things are going well, but as soon as something goes off track or someone tells you that you should do it another way, you go into a tailspin of doubting yourself? You might start thinking, *I'm not good enough. I'm not cut out for this. I can't do it.* Then, instead of doing what you want or need to do, you become unfocused and make choices that aren't right for you, which leaves you doubting yourself even more. The fear of failure is high, your goals take longer to reach, and you're more stressed out.

Perhaps you feel confident about an upcoming presentation but, as it gets closer, you start to doubt yourself. *What will they think of me? What if I forget what I want to say?* You put all your focus on the negative thoughts and how things could go wrong, and you miss the opportunity to focus your attention on how you want it to go and how things could go well. Or maybe you say no to someone to honour your boundary to leave work on time but you do it from a place of apologizing rather than leaning into your ability to make an empowering choice.

Confidence is a big word with a lot of meanings. If you ask ten people (even experts) how to be more confident or what confidence means, you'll likely get ten different answers. The dictionary definition is:

- The feeling or belief that one can rely on someone or something; firm trust
- The state of feeling certain about the truth of something
- A feeling of self-assurance arising from one's appreciation of one's own abilities or qualities.

See, confidence is a belief and feeling. This means you have more control over your confidence in any moment by changing your perspective, shifting how you feel, and mastering that mind game. You get to choose how you think about yourself and show up at any moment. This is how you can tap into confidence on demand—especially when you need it—by being more intentional with how you think about yourself and doing the things that help you *feel* more confident (we'll get to this in a moment).

When we think positively about ourselves, acknowledging our strengths and accomplishments, we fuel our self-confidence. Similarly, a stream of self-doubt, criticism and negative self-talk can erode our confidence. When we're more self-aware and mindful of our thoughts, it's easier to feel more confident in our choices, show up with more authenticity, and stop depending on the outside world to tell us how we should think or feel about ourselves.

Our mental dialogues shape our self-perception and, in turn, how we present ourselves to the world. If we believe we're capable, competent, and worthy, we act in ways that affirm these beliefs. When we believe in our abilities and view ourselves positively, we naturally feel more confident. Again, we build confidence as we take action and build competence, but the feeling or belief or mindset of confidence is what gets us out the door to that thing.

Why is this so important when it comes to creating balance in your life? If you're going to go against the grain and align your actions with your values, say 'no' more, and speak up about what you want and need, you're likely going to face a whole lot of doubts and fear—and other people telling you what you should or shouldn't do. This is normal! Tapping into more confidence in the moment will help you turn down the volume on these doubts, use your time and energy more wisely, and take action on the choices right for you.

In this chapter, we'll explore how you can access confidence on demand and feel more confident in yourself and your choices. But first...

The big secret

Do you secretly wish that you could speak up in meetings and not let the anxious feelings keep you from saying what's really on your mind? That you could feel good about your decisions and spend less time overthinking or second-guessing yourself? That you didn't let the fear of failure and doubts run through your mind until you receive feedback that you're hitting the mark? That you didn't feel like you have to pretend you have it all together or you look at others thinking, *I wish I was confident like that person*?

Here's what I can confidently tell you: so do others—even those people you look up to! Research shows that most people struggle with confidence and self-worth. Most people doubt themselves or feel like an imposter. Regardless of their skills or experience. I've never worked with a coaching client who didn't doubt themselves and wonder if they were good enough. I still experience doubts and imposter syndrome anytime I am stretching myself and out of my comfort zone, such as speaking on a stage.

There's nothing wrong with you! Or me! But all the overthinking and doubting ourselves takes up a huge amount of mental and physical energy, blocks action, and stops us from letting our authentic, best selves out to reveal what we're truly capable of.

The truth is that no one feels totally confident all the time or has it all together. To have confidence in ourselves, we must understand that our confidence WILL come and go. We must trust that we can figure things out, even when the doubts come up. Tapping into more confidence and turning down the volume on your doubts is a muscle you can build (this is mindfulness).

YOUR FEAR OF FAILURE

Want to know what it takes to have that deeper level of confidence in yourself, even when the fear of failure is high? The kind of confidence where you won't give up on what you really want just because someone said no or you didn't hit your goal or it seems too hard? The kind of confidence where you speak up in a meeting or stand up for what you believe to be right or aligned with your values, even though someone might not like it or judge you? The kind of confidence where you put yourself out there and make choices right for you—because you trust in your ability to handle whatever comes your way?

Real confidence is the willingness to put yourself out there and not let the fear hold you back. To be okay with messing up and getting it wrong sometimes, trusting that you'll figure it out and will be okay. That's where this inner confidence in yourself comes from—the ability to calm your mind amid the fears and doubts that WILL pop up.

The fears and doubts will be there, but the key is to make sure they're in the passenger seat and you're the driver.

This is the kind of confidence that helped me to stop overworking in my corporate career and to create a business that aligned with my values even though I wasn't necessarily competent yet. It's still the biggest thing I work on today when I speak to audiences. It's what I worked on while writing this book. I'm a full-blown introvert and a private person, and while it excites me to put myself out there, it also terrifies me. I'd never have written this book if I hadn't learned how to calm my fears and doubts.

This also comes with quieting your inner critic. The unhelpful voice in your head that points out everything that's wrong with you, focuses on every mistake, and confirms that you're not good enough. It makes you overthink and doubt yourself and fear you'll mess something up. And when the inner critic gets to be too loud, you end up not taking action on what really matters or ask the question. You allow your confidence to be eroded. The thing is, anytime you do something new or step out of your comfort zone, your inner critic will likely speak up. You can quiet that inner critic and tap into more confidence. Why does this matter?

Your confidence in yourself and your choices can significantly contribute to a more balanced life in several ways. You're more likely to:

- Make decisions that align with your values, needs, and true desires
- Use your time, attention, and energy more wisely
- Be better at setting boundaries and priorities
- Experience less anxiety and stress associated with self-doubt
- Believe in your ability to handle difficult situations
- Be open to trying new things and stepping out of your comfort zone—like saying no
- Speak up and share your ideas and positively influence others
- Live your life in a way that is meaningful to you, rather than paths dictated by others.

Anytime you take on a new challenge or stretch yourself or take back control of your days, it's normal for doubts and fears to pop up. If they don't, you might not be pushing yourself enough to grow. The most successful and balanced people know that their doubt will slow them down and undercut their performance and happiness if they let it get to be too loud. They understand that the fear of failure or worry about what other people think or doubts about making a choice that's right for them is only chipping away at their confidence and consuming their time and energy.

What's important is to be aware of those fears and doubts—acknowledge that they are there, balance them out by tapping into more confidence in the moment, and take the action you want to take.

But how do you do this?

TAP INTO YOUR CONFIDENCE

You've already learned how to shine your attention flashlight in a more helpful way. Here are a few other simple tools and mindsets you can use and actions you can take right now to put yourself in a better frame of mind to tap into confidence when you need it. You don't need to try all of these at once so, as with everything else in this book, pay attention to what stands out. Listen to your inner guidance.

Continue to get to know and trust yourself more. Continually learn about yourself and connect with what you do know about what matters to you. When you're clear on this, it's easier to let your choices come from within. Listen to your intuition. You know yourself better than anyone else does. You've already explored your values, boundaries, and who you want to be. Use this inner guidance to feel more confident in your choices.

Remember that a mindfulness practice will help you cultivate a different relationship with yourself. A non-judgmental, open, and observing stance will allow you to take a step back from all the unhelpful voices and pressures so you can go within and make choices more aligned with who you are.

Turn down the volume on your inner critic. Too many people let their inner critic lead the way—especially women. When you make choices that are in deeper alignment with your values and real priorities, that voice won't matter so much. You can also learn to quiet your inner critic with mindfulness (Chapter 7). This is about turning down the volume, just as you need to do with the worry and guilt. You do far more good things in a day than you realize, so put the focus on the wins and you'll feel more confident in yourself.

Leverage your strengths. Often, the default approach when dealing with people, performance, and ourselves is to focus on "what's wrong." When we put our attention on our strengths, however, we use our energy more effectively. We're truly at our best when we focus on what we're good at. Focusing on your strengths leads to a deeper confidence in your abilities (as well as to your best performance). Not to mention you'll be more strategic about how you use your time and energy.

Your strengths are the things that come naturally to you, not the things you wish you were good at. You'll feel more confident in yourself when you focus on that, rather than your perceived flaws and limitations.

Adopt the mindset *Either I'll win or I'll learn*. When you shift to this mindset—things will either work out the way you want them to or you'll get the lesson you need—it's easier to avoid putting all that pressure on yourself to be perfect. You can't win unless you put yourself out there and, even when things don't work out, there's always something to learn that will make you stronger next time.

This mindset keeps me moving toward my business goals. It helps me not to give up. There have been A LOT of flops, and things often take longer than expected, but this mindset helps me tap into my confidence (even with the fear of failure). And with this confidence, I know I can figure things out.

Reframe the situation and your thoughts. Again, anytime negative thoughts creep up (and they will), reframe. This doesn't mean ignoring how you feel or pretending everything is okay. It means recognizing that the story you tell yourself makes a difference in how you feel and the actions you take. For example, if you're freaking out and nervous, tell yourself you're excited and grateful. When your heart is racing, your brain doesn't know the difference between excitement and nervousness, so you can tell it a more empowering story. Or instead of thinking *I have to*, tell yourself *I choose to* or *I get to*. You'll feel more confident in those moments.

Instead of focusing on what you're doing wrong (which is not as bad as your brain makes it out to be), reframe the situation by reflecting on a time when you did a good job, when you did something challenging and it went well, or even on a time when you thought something would go terribly but it all worked out.

Remind yourself that you are absolutely capable.

Ask yourself empowering questions. This ties to the last one. Have you ever felt confident about something and then, the very next moment, doubted everything? I know I have! Your mind will go where you take it, so adjust where you focus your attention when the doubts come up. Remember, you choose where to shine your flashlight. Here are some questions to ask yourself when doubts come up.

- If I were confident in myself, what would I say or do? (This connects you to what your intuition is telling you.)

- What's a better way to see this? What's the opportunity or lesson for me?
- What am I really good at? What value do I bring? What are my strengths?
- If a best friend was going through this, what would I tell them?
- If I weren't worried about what people would think, what would I do?

By shifting your focus to something more positive and empowering when panic or doubts set in, you'll feel more confident in the moment, which will ultimately influence your outcomes.

Let go of what other people think. Easier said than done, I know. We often look for validation from others to boost our confidence, and receiving it can certainly make us feel more confident. But it's important to understand that we can generate confidence in ourselves anytime we need it. It all goes back to how we think about ourselves.

Be mindful of when you're gaining and losing confidence during your interactions with others, and then try not to do either, to avoid relying on someone or something else to decide whether to feel good about yourself. And the truth is, most people are doubting themselves and figuring it out too. You'll instantly gain confidence when you let go of worry about what other people think.

Detach from the outcome. I have a high amount of anxiety about things that scare me, whether it's speaking on stage or skiing with my kids. One strategy I've always found effective, even during my corporate career, is to detach from the outcome. This doesn't mean I'm disengaging from what I'm doing—I'm just letting go of what might happen.

Before I go into a meeting or speak on stage or while standing at the top of a ski hill, I tell myself, *Whatever will happen, will happen.* This helps me to completely let go. Otherwise, my anxiety would be so high that I wouldn't show up as my best self and I wouldn't be able to be present and enjoy the experience.

By detaching yourself from the outcome, you can access more confidence, presence, and enjoyment in the moment. (Though I still breathe a huge sigh of relief when we're done skiing for the day and everyone is okay!)

Be bold and courageous. Courage is a big factor in confidence. It's the ability to do what needs to be done, regardless of the perceived cost or risk. When you focus your attention on being courageous and bold, you shift your mindset from a passive state (self-doubt) to an active one (confronting challenges).

Each time we choose to be bold and courageous, we show ourselves our strength and resilience, which in turn nurtures our self-confidence. When we step out of our comfort zones, even in small ways, we prove to ourselves that we're capable of handling uncertainty and adversity. We learn to trust in our ability to cope.

This is the essence of real confidence. It's not about never feeling scared or unsure—it's about recognizing those feelings and moving forward anyway. This process of building confidence through boldness and courage is also much like exercising a muscle. The more we use it, the stronger it becomes.

On those days when you're struggling to feel confident in yourself, focus on being bold and do the thing anyway.

Make a list of what gives you confidence. This is a favourite of mine. We all know what confidence feels like. And we all have things that help us feel more confident. You probably have some tools and tricks that work for you. Tap into them more!

Write down everything that helps YOU feel confident and reminds you of your greatness. It might be a person who leaves you feeling good about yourself, a podcast, a string of words, a quote, an affirmation, a place, or a song. Write out at least ten of these things. Then, anytime you need a boost, you can go to that list. This way, you don't have to figure out anything in the moment when you need confidence. It's also helpful to be aware of what chips away at your confidence. Over the years, I've learned which people and messages do this.

Here are a few things that work for me: When I doubt myself, a particular song can turn it all around. On social media, I read things that leave me feeling good or challenge my thinking, and I'll scroll on by the posts that I know will leave me feeling down about myself and hurt my confidence. I'll also ask my husband for a pep talk when I need to be reminded of what I can do.

Just do the thing. What if on the other side of your fear of failure is everything you want? The more you push through your fears and doubts, the easier it gets to overpower them in the future. The more you hold back because you're scared, the easier it is to hold back the next time. Take action and figure it out as you go!

Again, pay attention to what works (and doesn't work) for YOU. What gives you confidence will look different from what gives others confidence. It's also important to pay attention to your words and how you speak to yourself and others.

COMMUNICATE WITH CONFIDENCE

Our ability to communicate with confidence is a crucial aspect of how we feel about ourselves, how we present ourselves to others, and how we're perceived by others. Our words and the way we express them can either reinforce our self-assurance or chip away at it. So, pay attention to your words, especially when you're saying no or making an empowered choice.

When we speak with conviction, avoiding undermining language, we not only boost our own confidence but also influence how others see us. For example, habitually apologizing for things that don't warrant an apology suggests that we're always in the wrong or seeking approval, which can diminish our authority (in our own eyes and others').

Here's what confident communication can sound like at work:

- "I appreciate your confidence in my abilities, and I won't be able to take on this new project without overextending myself. Let's discuss how we can redistribute the workload or adjust deadlines to make it manageable."
- "Honesty is really important to me, so I want to openly express my thoughts on this issue. I believe we should prioritize transparency in our team's communication."
- "While I understand the urgency of other tasks, my current priority is completing the project we agreed on last week. Let's revisit the timelines of these other tasks once this is accomplished."
- "I have some ideas on how we can use our time more effectively as a team, including a few meetings that could be revamped or that we don't need at all. Can we discuss these opportunities to free up our time?"

In your personal life, confident communication might sound like this:

- "I really enjoy spending quality time together. I'd love for us to plan a weekend getaway soon. It's important to me that we connect in this way."
- "I value our time together, and I also need some time to myself to recharge. Can we arrange our schedules so that I have some alone time each week?"
- "I would love to attend your event; however, I already have important plans this weekend with my family, so I won't be able to join you. Thank you for the invitation and I hope you have a wonderful time!"
- "I've been feeling a bit overwhelmed with the household tasks. I really value all you do, and it would mean a lot to me if we could share these other responsibilities more. Can we sit down and figure out a way to divide them? It would help me manage my time better, and I think it would make things easier for both of us. Your help with this is really important to me."

When we're mindful of our language, choosing words that reflect strength and positivity, we lift our own spirits and also inspire confidence in others. We showcase our capability. We teach ourselves that it's okay to ask for help and honour what we need and value.

This doesn't mean ignoring difficulties or pretending everything is perfect; rather, it's about choosing words that highlight our ability to cope and succeed.

I still work on my confidence daily. I work on not letting the fears and doubts hold me back. You'll always face people who say you should do something that's misaligned with your values. Remember: you have the ability to feel more confident in yourself and your choices. Let this guide you and you'll be more likely to stay aligned with what success looks like and feels like in your life, feel less stressed out, and take the bold action you want to take.

Self-Awareness and Action:
HOW CAN YOU TAP INTO MORE CONFIDENCE?

Take some time to think about what gives you confidence. Reflect on these questions and write out freely whatever comes up for you without judging yourself or overthinking.

- What's something you did in the past that you were quite fearful of doing? How terrifying does it seem now? What benefit did you gain from doing it?

- What's something you really want to do that you haven't shared with people? If you were feeling confident in yourself, what would you do?

- Where in your life are you letting worry about what people think or fear of failure hold you back? What would you have the confidence to do if you let this worry go?

- If you were to be more "you" in your everyday life, what would you do?

- What are your strengths? What are you really good at? What comes naturally to you? What is something that feels easy for you (that might be more difficult for others)? Put your focus there.

- What are ten simple things that help you to feel more confident? Write them out and keep that list nearby so you can tap into more confidence anytime you need it.

Be bold. If you were confident in yourself, what action would you take this week to create more balance in your life? Go do that!

Confidence lessens the fear of failure and anxiety about outcomes, which can help reduce your stress level and enjoy your everyday experience more. This is what we'll dive into next.

Chapter 11

EXPERIENCE MORE JOY AND LESS STRESS

"And then one day, I decided that hurry and stress were no longer going to be part of my life."

– BRENDON BURCHARD

Summer is my favourite time of year. We spend most of our time at the lake in July and August. My husband and I bought our first cabin when the kids were still babies, and even during my corporate career, I took most Fridays off in the summer. Every year a goal of mine is to have *the best summer ever*.

Initially, we had said that it would be nice to own a cabin one day when we could afford it, or maybe when we retired. But we also wanted to enjoy the cabin experience when the kids were younger, so we decided to just go for it and create the lake experience and joy we really wanted. The cabin we purchased was a crappy old fixer-upper and over the years we made it our own.

When I started my business, I designed it around being able to live at the cabin for the summer since I had that flexibility. Spending summers at the lake is part of my version of success and balance. It allows us to experience more joy in our life and influences my choices in what I say yes and no to. People will sometimes say to me, "Wow, you're so lucky to be able to spend summers at the lake. It must be nice." (It's definitely nice.) Or, "Life must be pretty easy with your own business." (Running a business is definitely not easy.)

I tell people that it's a *choice*.

Spending so much time at the lake in the summer is the result of being crystal clear on my values, boundaries, and priorities. It means saying no to a whole lot of things, even good things— including a $40K contract, which I turned down early in my business because the company wanted me to work in the city over the summer (even though the money would have been helpful and allow us to pay off some debt from buying that cabin!).

Living at the cabin in the summer means intentional choices each day. It's being laser-focused to do two or three hours of work early in the morning before we jump into a beach day (I swear I get more done this way than I do on some full workdays). It comes with letting go of comments other fellow entrepreneurs have said to me, such as, "If you were really dedicated to your business, you'd be available and work on your business more." It comes with being present in the everyday moments and enjoying my time instead of getting wrapped up in the stressors of the day. And it comes with an inner confidence and knowing about what I want for myself and my family and the choices I need to make for this to happen.

My bigger intention with spending summers at the lake or any other day is this: to experience more joy and less stress in my life. To have a deeper appreciation for the day and not stress (so much) about it all. An intention like this helps me (and can help you) to feel more balanced, and be present and *enjoy* life even when things are challenging.

I'm intentional about this now, but I didn't used to be.

Years ago, we went on a family vacation to San Diego with the kids. My husband and I were so stressed out from all the trip preparation and burned out from work that we fought for most of our vacation. We'd spent all this time and money getting ready for this big trip and then we didn't enjoy the time away! We were just as stressed out when we got home. Ever had that happen? Or maybe you experience higher stress levels leading up to a trip because you're cramming two weeks of work into one so you could leave for a few days. Or perhaps the stress of being away from work made you wish you hadn't scheduled your vacation. Maybe you come home feeling like you need a vacation after your vacation! You're experiencing more stress and less joy.

At the end of my corporate career, the main feedback I was getting from my colleagues was to smile. I would walk into a meeting and someone would say "Smile, Stacey". The ironic thing was that early in my corporate career, I worked with a director who rarely smiled. Someone told me he used to be a happy-go-lucky type but had been worn down over time. My cheery, upbeat, energetic, go-getter self said that would never be me. And there I was all those years later—not being intentional about enjoying the day.

Soon after I left, I did get back to feeling like my happier self (this didn't mean I didn't have bad days, but overall I lived with a daily intention to find the joy each day ... and smile). However, at the start of the pandemic, I went through a period where I found myself feeling blah every single day. This was that old habit I fell back into during the first few months of juggling online school with client calls, and not being able to be with people. I'd wake up with a sigh of *Let's just get through the day.*

One winter weekend at the lake, my husband and I were out for a walk. Strolling down an alley, I saw a sign on a cabin that proclaimed: *Today is a great day to be alive.* I immediately realized what was missing for me—appreciation for the day! Since that day, every single morning before I get out of bed, I say out loud to myself, *Today is a great day to be alive*. I then take a moment to feel true appreciation and gratitude. This is the single most important habit I have that helps me feel more joy for my day and keep my stress level in check. Even on the hardest day of my life—which I will share in the next chapter—I still repeated that affirmation when I woke up in the morning. This helped me appreciate that I was breathing and present for the day ahead, even knowing it would definitely not be a great day.

When we're not living with a daily intention and being mindful of how we want to feel and show up in our lives, it can be easy to fall into *Let's just get through it* and miss out on the joy.

THE MESSY LESSON AND KEY SHIFT

Feeling more balanced comes with being able to be present in and enjoy your daily experiences. To give yourself permission to do more of what gives you joy. To feel more positive emotions. To let go of the stress you're carrying around that's dampening your experience. To create the life and experiences you want.

> **It's up to you, and you alone, to decide to choose more joy and stress less, whether you're on vacation or having a regular workday. No one else will do this for you.**

This underscores the idea that we each have the power to choose our perspective and how we respond to our situation, regardless of external circumstances. Recognizing that you can decide to focus on joy and manage your stress effectively is crucial for your sense of balance, well-being, and mental health. Now, you might not have the kind of autonomy or resources to do everything you want. One big reason I didn't go back to a corporate career when asked to return was that I wouldn't be able to live at the lake for the summer (remote work wasn't a thing yet). Creating the balance you want in your life might mean making bigger moves, such as switching to a job with more flexibility or having the courage to ask for what you really want in your current role, e.g., a four-day workweek or Fridays off in the summer. It can also be finding even small ways to incorporate more joy and less stress into your days with your current situation, which makes a significant difference in how you experience it. Maybe you dedicate fifteen minutes a day to an activity you enjoy, or take short breaks during work to relax and listen to music you love.

The point is to stop simply going through the motions and be more intentional each day. To be more present and enjoy each day, even if life feels messy and chaotic.

MAKE FEELING GOOD A PRIORITY

You might have the best of intentions. You might be trying to do things differently. Maybe you've cut back on meetings to create some breathing space to get your work done but people keep booking up your calendar. Maybe you tried to put a morning routine in place but soon went back to checking emails or rushing around as soon as you got out of bed. Or maybe you love going for walks and have decided to walk outside every day but can never seem to find the time because you need to get to everyone else's needs first. You might find yourself thinking that tomorrow will be the day, but tomorrow turns out to be the same, and you're still feeling frustrated, overwhelmed, and worn out. Does any of this sound familiar?

This is what Rebecca, a client of mine, experienced. She was going through the motions, thinking that life was just busy and she had no choice, given her new demanding position as a director. Still, she was feeling run-down, she complained about work more than she wanted to, and she felt guilty for missing time with her kids (and for not enjoying the time she did have with them).

Rebecca had the best of intentions and *tried* to do things differently, and she still felt frustrated, overwhelmed, and worn out.

We spent time on topics you've already learned about in this book, such as self-awareness and connecting with values, and we also looked at what would help her to enjoy her days more. Very quickly, Rebecca finally started to make meaningful changes in her life.

Her biggest shift, which made everything possible, was this: instead of thinking of breathing space in her calendar, a morning routine, and walks as simply tasks on her to-do list, she began thinking of them as the things that "fill her up"—the habits that leave her feeling good and less stressed out. These are the things that give her energy. They make her days feel easier. This changed everything for Rebecca, and she finally started to stick to them.

We've already explored how happiness is a positive emotional state with feelings such as contentment, satisfaction, and joy in our daily lives and experiences. I see my joy and happiness as intertwined—the quiet joy I experience leaves me feeling happy each day. Our well-being encompasses positive emotions, as well our relationships, physical and mental health, and our sense of meaning.

Positive emotions are crucial in our happiness, performance and boosting our energy levels. They broaden our perspective, enhance creativity, and help us tap into more confidence, thereby directly influencing our ability to perform at our best—and enjoy our experiences. When we experience emotions such as joy, love, and gratitude, our mindset shifts from a narrow focus on problems to a wider view of possibilities; we see more solutions and engage more deeply with our work or activities. Moreover, positive emotions reduce stress.

Individuals who regularly experience positive emotions are found to be more resilient in the face of adversity, bounce back faster from setbacks, and are more likely to achieve their goals and higher levels of success. Positive emotions also enhance our connections with others. When we take care of ourselves and feel better, we can be there for others in a more meaningful way. I don't know about you, but I am far more present, patient, and pleasant with others when I am not running on empty or feeling stressed out. As well, people who exude positivity and optimism are often better at inspiring and motivating others and driving higher performance within teams.

Positive emotions don't just lift our mood. They promote a harmonious state of being. They help us to feel more centered and grounded, to have a calm and clear mind. They provide a stable foundation from which to approach life's challenges. They help us to experience more joy and less stress in our lives.

Positive emotions and our sense of balance

In essence, positive emotions aren't just pleasant to experience. They don't just offer temporary boosts of happiness or performance—they significantly contribute to a sense of balance in our lives. And when we feel more balanced, we're better equipped to make thoughtful decisions, pursue our goals with a clear vision, and be more patient and present with people. Remember, impatience can be a sign that you're out of balance.

Yet, the very things that help us feel good and take care of our well-being are often sacrificed to get the job done—making things way harder than they need to be. Many people tend to stay in a state of overwhelm, worry, and resentment rather than honouring what they need to increase their positive emotions and feel better. This can look like:

- Sacrificing sleep to meet deadlines or finish tasks
- Dropping regular exercise from a busy schedule even though exercise is crucial for maintaining physical health, managing stress, and improving our mood
- Overcommitting when it comes to work, which leads to impatience and less time spent with family and friends
- Ignoring mental health in the pursuit of working harder
- Being unable to disconnect from work
- Not investing in personal development and growth
- Overlooking basic self-care practices, such as eating well, hydrating, taking short breaks during work, and getting regular medical check-ups.

We won't do all the things that are good for us! There are always trade-offs with our time and energy and what's going on in our season of life. The key is to ensure that you prioritize more of what gives *you* joy and what helps you to feel less stressed. It's okay to make time for what feels good for YOU. In fact, it's imperative if you want to perform at a high level, better navigate life's ups and downs, and be happier and more balanced in your life.

But also know that when you're feeling overwhelmed or frustrated, it's okay. Every emotion is important. Don't ignore these emotions or stuff them down.

Our emotions point the way

Just as a compass points you in a certain direction, so can emotions. Emotions that feel good, such as joy and contentment, can let you know that what you're doing is beneficial or aligned with your values, while other emotions, such as overwhelm and frustration, can signal that something needs to be addressed or that you're off track in some way (e.g., your actions are misaligned with your values). When you pay attention, you can use your emotions to help guide your choices.

When I was impatient and fighting with my husband and kids each day, it was because I had way too much on my plate and I was exhausted and overwhelmed. On that vacation in San Diego, I was running on empty (as was my husband). And people felt it.

Feeling good is my priority these days. It doesn't mean I don't have bad days or that I don't feel overwhelmed or frustrated or that I exercise every day. I'm simply more intentional about enjoying each day, no matter what happens. Prioritizing what helps me to feel less stressed out, such as meditation, daily movement, and listening to music I love, is part of this. And when I'm feeling overwhelmed or frustrated or tired, I pay attention to what my compass is telling me instead of running myself down more.

Of course, while taking a breather when your frustrations or overwhelm get the best of you can be helpful, it's not a longer-term fix. For the long term, what's important is to keep your tank more on the full side.

YOU'RE TOO WISE TO BE ON EMPTY

One day, my husband took the car that I usually drive, and when I used it the next day, the fuel gauge was on orange, almost empty. I was late to my appointment because I had to fill up. I called him and said, "We're way too old and wise to be living on orange!" Which got me thinking that we're way too old (and wise) to be living on orange when it comes to our own fuel tanks.

Think of your energy level as a fuel tank. People often wait until their tanks are empty to make a change or take a break or do something to care for themselves—but it's way more effective, and feels way better, to keep your tank on the fuller side. Even if life is in a demanding season, keeping your tank in the top half can make all the difference in how you navigate that challenging time and show up for others. It's way easier to fall into more negative emotions and unhelpful reactions, feel your confidence dipping, and let the overwhelm paralyze you when your tank is near empty.

There are things you can do each day to fill your tank—and drain it. To experience more joy or less. To feel less stressed out or even more stressed out. Reflect on these questions (they are also at the end of this chapter).

- What gives you joy and energy?
- What does a full tank look like for you? What does half a tank look like? What does an empty tank look like?
- How do you know when you're at a half tank? Pay attention to the warning signals and refuel before you're on the empty side!

You likely already have ideas about what a great day looks like for you (go back to Chapter 4 on boundaries). Do more of this! What drains your tank? Do less of that!

You might look at others and think, *They seem to have a bigger tank than I do. Is something wrong with me?* People do have different energy levels. And sometimes it depends on the season of life you're in. I have more mental and physical capacity to write this book now than I would have had when my kids were toddlers, for example. But can we all look for ways to better manage our energy? Yes.

Ideally, you keep your tank on the fuller side. But if you're on empty now? It's time to take care of you and honour what YOU need to feel and be your best. It's time to put more gas in your tank.

BOOST POSITIVE EMOTIONS AND FEEL BETTER

When you engage in practices and activities that bring joy and positive emotions, you feel better and enjoy life more. This will look different for different people or even depending on the day. Here are some ways to increase your positive emotions and counterbalance the stress and challenges you face each day. *More* joy and *less* stress.

Protect your joy and peace. Setting boundaries doesn't just protect your time—it's crucial for preserving your joy and peace. Essentially, boundaries reflect what you will and won't tolerate. By setting clear boundaries, you protect your mental and emotional energy from being drained by others' demands or negativity. This helps you maintain a sense of well-being and reduces stress, as you're less likely to feel overwhelmed or taken advantage of. This can look like saying no to attending a family event out of obligation or not continuing a meeting with a colleague if they aren't being respectful.

Moreover, boundaries allow you to honour your needs and refuel. They give you the space necessary to enjoy your personal time and nurture your inner peace. The things that make you feel good are just as important as the things other people need, so make space for them.

Do what gives you joy and energy. For years, I really wanted a hot tub but my husband wasn't on board. Finally, one day I came home from work and announced, "If we're going to work this hard, I want to spend our money on what gives us joy! I want to buy a hot tub." Kenton agreed and, that day, I went out and bought a hot tub. We both love it and still use it most days ten years later. It's how we decompress after the workday or enjoy some time together. Similarly, we purchased our summer cabin because we knew it would give us joy. We didn't want to wait until we retired or were financially in a better place to experience it. These days, I think of it as, *I'm not keeping up with the Joneses—I'm keeping up with My Joys.*

Doing what gives you joy doesn't have to involve buying things or doing something big. I also find joy in being alone with a cup of coffee in the morning and in playing a game of basketball with my kids. These not only give me joy, these are the very things that give me energy for my day. It's easy to dismiss doing things that fill your tank as: *I don't have time* or *I can't afford it.* But imagine what your life would be like if you gave yourself permission to have more experiences that give you joy. Listen to a song. Have some alone time. Take the vacation you've been talking about. Whatever gives you a boost of joy and feels good.

Brainstorm and write down ten small, simple things that give you joy or leave you feeling good. A few examples: listening to music, going for a walk, reading a book, having coffee with a friend, calling someone you love, watching a funny video, snuggling with your kids, spending an evening out. Also consider some bigger experiences that would give you joy. Can you make a plan to make these things happen?

Add something into your day that gives you joy when you're feeling negative, overwhelmed, and frustrated to cultivate emotions that are more positive.

Give joy to others (and don't steal their joy). Making someone else's day a little brighter can not only boost their positive emotions but yours as well. Along with gratitude (more on this shortly), it's one of the simplest, most powerful things you can do. Take a few minutes of your day to ask someone how they're doing, buy a cup of coffee for a stranger, send an unexpected email to praise a team member, be patient with someone struggling, or do something helpful for another.

How can you give joy to others? Kindness goes a long way.

Also be mindful to let people enjoy what they enjoy. I'll always remember what that neighbour said to me when I asked her if her teenager was too old to have a stuffed animal: "Who am I to take away someone else's joy?" This hit me like a lightning bolt and still guides my choices today.

Greet the people you love as if you haven't seen them in ten days. This has been a game-changer for me. Years ago, I was introduced to this idea in a book on stress-free living and have been doing it ever since.

You know how you feel when you see your kids or someone you love for the first time in ten days? Greet your kids or your partner like this every morning or when you get home from work or they get home from school. For at least fifteen minutes, resist the urge to be critical or get frustrated with them and just be so darn happy to see them. Fifteen minutes like this each day can change any relationship for the better by being more connected, present . . . and patient.

Be kinder to yourself. One essential way to fill your tank is to be kinder to yourself and practice self-compassion. Again, sometimes things will go wrong. For instance, you might miss an important deadline, fail to get a big client, make a mistake, say yes to something you know you should have said no to, or get impatient with your loved ones. How do you usually react to such things?

It's far too common to be hard on yourself: *What's wrong with me? Why can't I do this? Why me?* A negative judgment is often the automatic response to failure. Forgiveness and compassion are missing. And this compassion is of extreme importance because it has the power to transform all that negativity.

While the uncompassionate voice says *What's wrong with me? How could I have let this happen?*, the compassionate voice says *What happened has happened. You're human, just like everyone else. Another lesson learned. Next time, you can try something different.* This is acceptance, which is a key element of mindfulness.

Let go of the drama. It's so freeing when you let go of all the drama. When you don't let self-doubt and worry eat at you, you don't treat others poorly when you're in a bad mood, you don't get caught up in complaining and gossip, and you don't blame others when you should really be asking yourself: *What am I doing to make it better?*

When you do get caught up in the drama of worrying if you're good enough or arguing with others or complaining, you waste mental energy that could be put to more positive and productive use. Decide that you just don't have room for it anymore because you're using your time and energy more wisely. Let go of the stress. You'll set a positive example for others.

Put some fun time on your calendar. Add something you enjoy to your calendar and stick to it as you would to any other commitment. Promising yourself a reward for completing a project or a busier season at work can give you motivation to see it through—a light at the end of the tunnel. Although you don't need to accomplish something or get things done to do something fun for yourself! Book your winter vacation, plan an evening out with friends, or schedule a massage. Whatever fun looks like for you.

Seeing these things in your schedule will help you to enjoy the days leading up to them more and experience more joy when they happen. My summers at the lake are a big milestone for me each year and I protect them as much as possible.

Disconnect (especially on vacation). Since many of us don't "turn off" as often as we should in our day-to-day lives, it's more important than ever to disconnect from our work during our downtime and vacations. Continual engagement with work, especially mentally demanding tasks, can lead to mental fatigue. Remember, our minds and bodies weren't designed to be on 24/7. Disconnecting allows your brain to rest and recover, which reduces stress. Make room for joyful, rejuvenating activities. It will help you be more effective when you do return to work. And when you're not preoccupied with work, you can be more present while engaging in your personal activities. We often spend a lot of money to go on trips just to get a break from our busy lives, so why not take full advantage of the escape? Start by putting that phone away!

Minimize your stressors. By now, this should go without saying. You need to honour your boundaries to protect your time and energy and create space for what you need to feel and be your best. Go back to Chapter 4 and see where you could add another boundary that works for you to give you more of those great days. If you haven't already, you might want to identify one or two of those daily pressure-cooker moments we explored in the chapter on stepping out of overwhelm, and do something about them to lessen the stress.

Smile. While there tends to be some pushback on this advice, it's something I do every day. Even on days I don't feel like it. Smiling sends a signal to your brain that can kick-start a happier feeling and help put you in that state. I also like to think maybe my smile will brighten someone else's day. Do what feels right for you.

HUNT FOR THE GOOD AND *FEEL* GRATITUDE EACH DAY

This might just be the most important way to keep your tank filled and increase positive emotions. Many people go about their day without truly appreciating what they *do* have. Instead, they spend a great deal of time feeling stressed out about what they *don't* have, or stuff that doesn't really matter. I used to do this often, and still fall into it at times. But when you truly feel the emotion of gratitude—as in, you don't just say thanks but really *feel* grateful—your energy changes. You become happier and more resilient. You respond better to stress.

Most of us are so fortunate yet spend so much of our time focusing on the small stuff we're unhappy with. As mentioned, the habit that makes the single biggest difference in my life is saying *Today is a great day to be alive* when I wake up in the morning. Gratitude is the simplest, most powerful feeling you can cultivate to experience more positive emotions and enjoy your days more. And everyone has the capacity to do so.

Put the focus on what you're receiving and the good things around you. Try writing down three good things that happened to you each day or starting your day with a thank-you and a gratitude practice.

Even on the tougher days

It's easier to be grateful when things are going well, but you can always reframe a situation with gratitude. Here are a few examples of how to do this:

- If you feel disappointed that you didn't get the promotion you wanted, you can choose to focus on what's good about the position you have now (or on the fact that you even have a job)
- Rather than starting your day dreading everything you have to do, you can choose to feel grateful you have this day and then consider how you can make the most of it
- When you're feeling impatient and not present with your kids, pause to recognize that time goes fast
- Transform "I hate that I have to ..." into "I'm grateful I get to ...".

Little shifts in your perspective can change everything. And for a little more perspective, let's face it: a bad meeting or bad performance review or losing your job or someone being disrespectful to you—these things aren't that bad in the bigger picture.

On tougher days or when I'm upset about something, I ask myself: *If this were my last day alive, would I be happy with who I'm being?* or *What if everything I had today was gone tomorrow?* These questions instantly give me perspective. They center me and can put me in a feeling of gratitude almost instantly.

So, what if everything you have today was gone tomorrow? How can you be grateful for what you have now? Start hunting for the good and see the difference for yourself.

Start to prioritize what gives you joy and leaves you feeling good, as these things will fill YOU up and give you the energy you need to tackle your day. And do less of what stresses you out and drains your energy. You'll make better decisions, be more effective at work, and be more patient and present. You'll be kinder to others, stay out of the drama, and experience less negative thinking and emotions. And you'll have more energy throughout the day instead of feeling run-down and exhausted.

Self-Awareness and Action:
WHAT GIVES YOU MORE JOY AND LESS STRESS?

Give yourself permission to feel more joy and less stress. It won't make things perfect, but see how your experience shifts when you bring this intention into each day. Reflect some more on these questions and write out freely whatever comes up for you.

- What does a full tank look like for you? What about half a tank? Or an empty tank? What does your fuel tank look like right now?

- What helps you fill your tank and gives you energy and joy? Brainstorm and write out ten things that help you feel good. This is what you CAN do.

- What drains your tank or stresses you out? These are things you can do less (or differently).

- What else helps you feel good and boosts positive emotions?

- What is something you've been wanting that would give you joy? What would you like to not do that's stressing you out? Can you make a plan and go for it?

Be bold. What is one thing you could do today to experience more joy and less stress? Just do it!

As you learn to calm your busy mind, be present, and enjoy your days more, you'll *feel* more balanced in your life. You'll be more mindful of where your attention is and whether the choices you're making align with your values, boundaries, and priorities. You'll be better able to step out of the overwhelm, and you'll be more focused and productive (and you'll feel better). You'll free up some time and mental energy normally spent on worry, guilt, and doubting yourself (which we all do). You'll feel more confident in your choices and experience more joy and less stress.

I hope that you're internalizing the idea that it's hard to be your best when you're exhausted and spread thin, and I hope that you're feeling more empowered to make time and be present for what really matters, both in your work and your personal life.

Remember that the changes in your life don't need to be huge and sweeping. The small, day-to-day intentional choices will build your mindfulness muscle and can make a big difference. You don't have to do it all! This book is designed to help you figure out what helps you to be and feel more balanced in your life. One step at a time.

In the final part of this book, we'll explore how you can be your best self for yourself and others even with messy life—to *stay* balanced. You'll learn how to navigate tougher times with more ease and resilience, balance being there for others and making yourself a priority, and live your balanced, and bold, life.

We'll start with what to do when life throws you a curveball.

PART 3

Be Your Best for Yourself and Others (Even with Messy Life)

Chapter 12

NAVIGATE TOUGHER TIMES WITH MORE EASE AND RESILIENCE

*"Life doesn't get easier or more forgiving,
we get stronger and more resilient."*

– STEVE MARABOLI

My mom fell suddenly and seriously ill in August 2021. The kids and I were still living at the lake for the summer and immediately returned to the city. After being with my mom and dad at the hospital for a couple of days, I shifted into full-on juggling mode, spending time with her, working, kids, and the rest of my life.

Each weekday, I'd do some work and personal responsibilities in the morning and then travel forty-five minutes to the hospital (in another city) to be with her for the afternoon and evening. Then I'd drive back home. After a couple of weeks of this, she was doing somewhat better. She was told she could make a full recovery and could return to her home, which was a couple of hours away from where I lived.

While I didn't see her much once she went home, I talked to her often and did a lot of research on her illness. A full recovery didn't seem likely, and I silently grappled with the possibility that we might only have a year or two left with her. Then, in late September, she came to stay with me and my family for a few days while my dad was away. She was worse than I'd expected. I'd thought she was improving, but she clearly wasn't.

My mom didn't want me to take the week off work while she was staying with us, so I'd work in the mornings and check in with her between client sessions and take care of what she needed. In the afternoons, we'd spend time together when she was up for it, and I'd do errands and care for her. I was going through the day thirty minutes at a time, switching between client calls, spending a few minutes with her, and wiping away my tears.

I wanted to clear my calendar, but my mom said she'd feel guilty if I took the time and insisted she didn't want to be a "burden." So, I balanced time with her and with work. I navigated the days calmly and stayed present with what I was doing as best as possible at each moment. She was clearly not doing well, and I wanted to take her back to the hospital or to see a doctor, but she refused to go. Other than with my husband, I haven't talked about or shared with anyone what this experience was really like (you're getting the very high-level version here).

That weekend, when she was back home, she seemed worse when I talked to her. We were all concerned and figuring out what to do.

On Monday morning, I wrestled with a decision: do I drive two hours (one-way) to check in on her and see if I could get her to see a doctor? It wasn't convenient to go. I had a full week of work (especially since I'd pushed some things out from the weeks before), and the kids had activities and appointments. And my mom did NOT want me to come—she was very clear about this and didn't want any help. If she had wanted me to come, the decision would have been easy, and I would have gone. But she didn't, so I felt conflicted about what to do.

While I was driving down a busy street after dropping the kids off at school that Monday morning, the tears and stress about the situation and what to do bubbled over. When I'm stressed out or struggling, I'll ask myself, *What would I say to or ask a client?*

I remember this next moment so vividly. I pulled over to the side of the road and asked myself:

> ***What is my number one value? What is most important to me above all else, and what choice will reflect the person I want to be?***

That value is being present with others—especially when they need me the most. The decision was instantly crystal clear to go be with her. My mind also wandered back to that lesson I'd learned all those years earlier when my beloved dog Tazer died. *You might not get this time back. You need to be present for what matters most.*

I cancelled my meetings, packed up, and let my husband know he'd have to figure out how to take care of the things I'd been planning to do with the kids and on the household front. Within the hour I was on the road.

Tuesday morning, my dad and I got my mom to go to the hospital. Wednesday morning, we found out her organs were failing and she was no longer responsive. Thursday morning, October 7, she died with my dad, my siblings, and me by her side. It wasn't a year or two we had with her. It was a few, short days. She was sixty-four years old.

Even though that was the hardest time in my life (so far), I also thrived in all the ways I could. It was a season for me where life looked very different from usual, and I was definitely tipping more into the out-of-balance side of things. It was also another reminder of the importance of maintaining a sense of balance in our lives and within ourselves (as much as we can) and of the power of the perspective and tools I share with my clients—and now with you— and what I live each day.

THE MESSY LESSON AND KEY SHIFT

This experience reinforced just how important it is to be present and to live in a way that's aligned with our values. I was with my mom when it mattered most, and that's time together that I never would have been able to get back. The "old me" would have been too wrapped up in catching up on work and other responsibilities to drop everything and go see her on that Monday.

It also reinforced for me that it's easier to navigate the tougher times when you take care of yourself. From August to October that year, while I was juggling *way* more than usual, I still honoured my boundaries and didn't work in the evenings or on weekends to catch up because I knew I needed time to recharge and reset. I took as much off my plate as I could with work, and prioritized serving existing clients, giving myself three to four hours a day to focus on what mattered the *most* and let go of the rest. I said no to new opportunities and I kept things as simple as I could. I also honoured what I needed for myself to keep fuel in my tank, such as going for a daily walk, practicing gratitude, and taking time alone each morning.

> **It's easier to go through tougher times when you honour what you need, focus on what really matters to you, and make choices that are a reflection of who you want to be.**

While I still felt as if I were struggling to juggle it all, I also knew that it would have been so much harder if I hadn't done the things that helped me feel better. *While I definitely wasn't at a full tank, I never got below half.* I have no doubt that this is what enabled me to go through the days more calmly, with presence, show up in my relationships in the way I wanted and still appreciate the small moments of joy (for the most part).

I also compartmentalized. When I was working, I focused on that and when I was with my mom, I focused on her. I practiced mindfulness to stay present, accept what was happening, and turn down the volume on the worry and guilt. I felt what I needed to feel and gave myself (lots of) space for that too. Everything you've learned in this book I lived each day.

Now, there were also days when I did not handle a situation well or my frustration got the best of me with someone. This is understandable when we are more run down, and grief can come out in all sorts of ways. And there are some choices I made that I wish I hadn't. That's the thing about hindsight—it's a clearer picture looking backward because we have more information—we know how the story ends. But we can't change what happened in the past. What we can do is graciously accept the lessons. We can shift our perspective and hunt for the good. We can focus on what's within our control and let go of what's not.

We can take care of ourselves and be present with what is now.

RESILIENCE AND BALANCE ARE INEXTRICABLY LINKED

It's inevitable. Life will throw you curveballs. There will be more challenging days or seasons in your life. Even during these tougher times—especially during these times—whether you're struggling with your workload or caring for a sick family member or you lost your job or dealing with whatever challenge life is throwing at you—it's so important to be present with whatever is going on and live in a way that's aligned with your values, honour what you need, and make choices that reflect the person you want to be. Being kind to yourself (and granting yourself grace when you don't). To keep your sense of balance as much as you can.

Often, though, when things get tough, people ignore the very things that help them feel better. In doing so, they run themselves down more, lose perspective, and sacrifice what truly matters most to them, which leaves them feeling even more stressed out, more exhausted, and more conflicted. Their well-being, performance, and relationships all end up suffering. And the hard times feel even harder ... and you feel even more out of balance.

"Resilience and balance go together like peanut butter and jelly!" This popped out of my mouth while I was facilitating a resilience workshop with a leadership team about a year after my mom died. I'd never made the comparison before but, in that moment, it was such a perfect, simple way to think about it.

Resilience isn't about just toughing it out, which is what the old me thought. It's the ability to flexibly deal with the negative or challenging experiences you face, both the big setbacks *and* the small daily stressors, and to learn the lessons and grow stronger from them. It's much harder to navigate those setbacks and the daily stressors when your tank is empty or you feel as if you're sacrificing what really matters to you. And when you're more balanced, your tank isn't on empty and you have time and presence for what really matters.

To be more resilient, you need to take better care of yourself and what matters to you. To be more balanced, you need to better navigate the tougher times and daily stressors.

When you give yourself permission to honour your values, boundaries, and priorities, say 'no' more, calm your busy mind, experience more joy—everything we've covered up to this point—you'll naturally be more resilient. What might resilience and balance look like together in your everyday life and messier moments?

- Living and leading with your values and what really matters to you, especially in tougher times
- Being able to let go of anxious thoughts about your day and to-do list when you wake up in the morning
- Getting your kids out the door and yourself to work on time while remaining calm and patient (especially when the kids aren't so calm)
- Being present in a meeting even though your last conversation did NOT go well
- Stepping out of overwhelm by focusing on what matters most in the moment instead of thinking about the twenty other things you need to do
- Leaving work on time and ignoring that unhelpful inner voice that's saying, *You didn't do enough*
- Noticing you're complaining about a situation and then deciding to focus on what you can control instead
- Letting go of what's outside your control, such as worrying about worst-case scenarios or how other people might react to you (thereby freeing up a whole lot of mental energy)
- Enjoying your personal time without being distracted by worries about tomorrow
- Honouring what you need to fill your tank so you can better navigate it all—and paying attention when you feel as if you can't do these things (and then doing these things).

Now, you might already be better at taking care of yourself and balancing your work and personal time in a regular week (which is awesome), but what about those weeks when so many things seem to be going wrong? Your kid gets sick, your spouse is out of town, you're behind on a project, and you spilled coffee on your favourite shirt. Do you still take care of yourself and stay balanced and centered? Or do you end up feeling more stressed out, more frustrated, and even further behind?

Remember, you have a choice.
You're the captain of your boat.

Life is full of events and situations beyond our control. People demand more than we can give, loved ones face illnesses, and responsibilities pile up. It can get tough, messy, and overwhelming. But remember, YOU are in charge of how you show up. You can wait for things to improve. Or you can take the helm and navigate your days with more intention, ease and resilience.

What can make all the difference is being able to navigate the ups and downs with more calm—and even joy.

Much of what we've already explored contributes to your resilience, such as self-awareness, living your values, and choosing different thoughts and perspectives. It's also important to know that no matter your current situation, *you're already resilient*. You've already been showing up for yourself and others and doing your best. We can also tap into more resilience in ourselves.

So what can help you be even more balanced and resilient, both during the bigger, tougher times in your life and in the face of the smaller, everyday stressors?

OPTIMISTIC PERSPECTIVE

Optimism is a huge factor in your resilience. It's belief in a positive future and that things will get better. People sometimes think that optimism and positivity are being unrealistic, but this shift in perspective is often about being **more** realistic—we tend to see things worse than they are or believe that one challenge will undermine everything or last indefinitely.

Being optimistic doesn't mean that you pretend everything is okay or that you don't acknowledge when you're struggling. It means being able to look at a situation and make the best of it, even though it's tough. It means noticing where you have a choice and looking for the good. When you're optimistic, you adopt the mindset that there's something you can do and hold the belief that things can get better.

You can be going through a hard time **and** remain optimistic. You can struggle **and** thrive. You can refill your tank when you need.

FOCUS ON WHAT YOU CAN CONTROL

It's worth repeating: While you don't have control over everything that's happening around you, you do have control over how you view and respond to what's happening. This shift in focus will empower you to take steps forward rather than stay paralyzed by uncertainty or external circumstances or let your struggles weigh you down and hide your best self.

Your thoughts, attitude, words, and actions are within your control. Your boundaries, how you treat others, and where you put your time and energy are within your control. Whether or not you ask for help is within your control. The choices you make are within your control.

Again, remind yourself that you have a choice and focus on what you can do.

You can regain a feeling of control by taking small actions that use your energy in a more positive and productive way. Ask yourself: *What CAN I do? What small step forward can I take? What's the lesson here for me for next time?*

Today, when faced with a tough situation, I tell myself to either take action on it or let it go (especially if I've determined that it's out of my control). For example, if I'm frustrated with someone, I'll either speak up and say something (take action) or be mindful not to complain or ruminate on it (let it go). I avoid getting stuck in "the middle place" of complaining or worrying while not actually doing anything that might make the situation better. I also focus on what's always within my control: how I show up.

Focusing on what you can control not only serves your resilience, you will use your time and energy far more wisely.

I had a client, Michael, who was feeling stressed out and not handling tougher situations at work well as a senior leader. We explored his values, and he realized that he showed up well most of the time, but in the more stressful situations, he didn't show up as the caring and patient leader he was at his core. His frustration revolved around other leaders' actions. The questions *How am I showing up?* and *How do I want to show up?* felt so simple, but profound to him. They reminded him that he could choose to focus on what was within his control and align his actions with his values.

LET GO OF WHAT YOU CANNOT CONTROL

One of the most freeing things you can do is to let go of what's outside of your control. This ties with calming your mind, being present, and practicing mindfulness and acceptance. Recognize the limits of your influence then intentionally choose to stop giving your attention, effort, and energy to what's outside of your control. Shift the beam of your flashlight.

This might mean letting go of what happened in the past (there's nothing you can do to change it) or other people's hurtful comments or complaining about a situation that you cannot change. The happiness of other people, the weather, external factors—these things are out of your control. The power of letting go is the recognition that expending energy on these factors leads to unnecessary stress, anxiety, and a sense of powerlessness. By consciously releasing our grip on the things that are outside of our control, we free up mental and emotional resources that we can use to focus on what matters more. It also feels much better.

MANAGE THE "IN BETWEEN" TIMES WITH MORE EASE

We all experience the "in between" stage as we go through a transition from something old to something new. Maybe you know what really matters to you but are still working on letting go of what matters less. Maybe you're trying to stick to a boundary to protect your personal time but are still learning to leave work on time. You could be working on being patient and present with your kids in the everyday moments but your frustration still gets the best of you some days. You are in a transition time now as you start to create more balance in your life. Perhaps you're going through a change in your career or joining a new team or experiencing grief.

In the times of transition, you know where you're headed (or at least have a sense), but you're not there YET. In these times, try to be even more mindful of how you're showing up and what you need. Doing so will help you to move through the transition with more grace and resilience. To appreciate things as they are and embrace the messiness as you grow.

You might choose to fight the messiness, stress out about it, or wish it were different. Or you can choose to be open to what's possible and keep moving forward.

I used to go through times of change with the assumption that they'd be super stressful. And guess what? They were. My "wish" came true. Now, I set the intention to go through them with more patience, calm, and grace. This means giving myself more space for the transition. Space for the fear and uneasiness. Space to feel gratitude and be excited about what's next. Space for grief and opportunity. Space to be present for all of it.

I give myself permission to let go of the old to make room for the new. To trust that things will get better and that I'll be okay and that there's something better on the horizon.

When we believe in a positive future and keep an optimistic outlook, we can move through transition times with more ease. And by embracing what we can control and letting go of what we cannot, we can cultivate a more balanced and resilient approach to life—and an ability to thrive even in the harder times. This also comes with learning how to get better at navigating the messier moments, such as when something unexpected happens, things go wrong, or you're short on time.

GET BETTER AT FLEXING IN YOUR DAY

In fast-paced everyday life—where each minute can carry its own set of demands—feeling balanced can often feel like walking a tightrope. To flex is to adjust and adapt as needed to your week or your day or the next five minutes, especially when the unexpected happens.

Learning to flex better allows us to navigate life's unpredictability with more calm and ease. It's reprioritizing as necessary, to get closer to the heart of what really matters. It's compartmentalizing and being fully present with the current moment. And this requires mindfulness to flow better with daily life and the messier moments that *will* happen.

On fuller days when I'm juggling work and personal demands, and something unexpected happens such as an impromptu visit from a family member or a project going off the rails, those days often come down to the minute for me. One more minute to get out the door to drive the kids to school. One more minute to finish getting ready before a client call. One more minute to finish a presentation before going into a two-hour virtual workshop with a team. I compartmentalize—*What is most important in the next five minutes?*—and focus on that. Over time, I've learned how to be present and calm in these minutes and not stress out (too much). My approach isn't perfect by any means, but I handle the unexpected days way better than I used to.

When we're better able to flex in the moment and ride the waves of our day, we can reduce our stress levels and feel more balanced within. We can shift our focus from the uncontrollable to mastering our inner balance (even when life feels tougher).

With an ability to adapt, we can approach each minute not as a source of stress but as a valuable part of our experience. And we're more likely to show up as our best selves.

Balance and resilience are two areas I focus on a lot with clients and my business. To me, they have EVERYTHING to do with each other. It's easier to go through the harder times when you honour what you need, focus on what really matters to you, and make choices that reflect the person you want to be.

I'm one-hundred-percent certain I wouldn't be as balanced if I weren't able to navigate the tougher times and daily stressors with more ease and resilience. Alone time supports my balance and resilience, and is something I prioritize even more these days since my mom died. It gives me space when I'm not responsible for anyone else's needs. It's when I can distance myself from others' voices so I can better hear my own intuition. It's time set aside when I fill my own tank. I read a book or meditate or do something that brings me joy. So I can better navigate whatever the day or week brings.

Looking back, I can see that when my mom got sick, I could have—and likely should have—taken more time off work (even though I'd cut my hours a lot already). My clients were so wonderful and understanding. But I had this story in my head: *People are paying me, so I have to show up. I don't have anyone to delegate to. It's just me and my business.* We learn our messy lessons as we go. I'm now working on hiring a right-hand person so that not everything falls on me. We might get our lessons in hindsight, but we can use them to shape our future.

No matter how tough life might get or how much responsibility you're facing, it's vital to take care of you, so you can navigate the tougher times with more ease and resilience.

Self-Awareness and Action:
WHAT SUPPORTS YOUR RESILIENCE AND BALANCE?

Reflect on these questions and write out freely whatever comes up for you without judging yourself or overthinking.

- Check in again: How are you *really* doing? What are you struggling with the most? How can you take better care of yourself so that you can navigate the tougher times better?

- As you go through a big setback or face a daily stressor, how are you showing up? How could you show up in a way that's better aligned with your values and who you want to be? Where can you grant yourself more grace and space as you go through this time?

- What frustrating situation could you take a more optimistic perspective on? What's an optimistic way to think about creating balance in your life?

- What situation currently feels difficult for you? List all the aspects of the situation that are within your control. What CAN you do? Then list all the aspects that are beyond your control. What can you let go of?

- What other actions might support your resilience and sense of balance? Brainstorm a few ideas.

Be bold. What is one thing you can do this week that would support your resilience and sense of balance? This will help make the tougher moments easier to navigate.

It can sometimes be extra challenging to remain balanced and resilient when you need to be there for others. This is what we'll dive into next to better balance being there for others and making yourself a priority too.

Chapter 13

MAKE YOURSELF A PRIORITY AND BE THERE FOR OTHERS

*"Taking care of myself doesn't mean 'me first.'
It means 'me, too.'"*

– L.R. Knost

During the pandemic, I put everything I'm sharing with you into serious practice. I had to work on my mindset, be more intentional to stay aligned with my values, and ensure I was focusing on the real priorities each day. I had to calm my mind, remain present, and be more resilient with the daily stressors.

Especially when it came to the blurred boundaries between work and home life. You see, I was great at keeping my work and family time separate, thanks to my strong boundaries. I rarely work evenings or weekends because I want my days to have similar rhythm as my husband and kids, and space for my personal time too. I thrive with more structure in my routine and room for flexibility.

But I also kept those firm boundaries because mixing work and family *really* stressed me out. When I tried to focus on both at the same time, I felt like I did a crappy job at both. So I just avoided this entirely with my excellent boundaries. Juggling work and kids simultaneously is an area of my life that I'd never learned to navigate with more ease and less stress because, up until the pandemic, I avoided it as much as possible.

Well, that all changed (as I'm sure it did for you) when work and home life became seriously blurred. I already worked from home, with the kids doing online school, and my husband working from home, too. We all had to figure out how to navigate the day and our new reality. I felt out of balance, but this time the other way—too much family time and not enough space for my work.

During those first few months, we experienced many ups and downs and some funny (and not so funny) moments.

My kids used my business Zoom account to visit with friends and, at some point, they all changed their user names to their *Fortnite* names. Well, I didn't know this.

For the next few weeks, I delivered several Zoom presentations to various companies and teams on resilience and how to thrive even when you're struggling. Some of these presentations were attended by more than one hundred people. I also do all my one-on-one coaching sessions on Zoom. Whenever I met with one executive coaching client, *Outlaw Munch* would come up on our screen and we'd jokingly ask each other, "Who is Outlaw Munch?" I thought that was his Zoom account name—and apparently, he knew it was mine. Yep, I still had no idea! With so much going on, it just didn't register.

Finally, one day, as I was about to start presenting to a group of sixty-five people, someone asked me, "Are you Outlaw Munch?"

I gasped out loud and said, "I AM OUTLAW MUNCH!"

For eight weeks, I'd been presenting and commenting with this username. I couldn't believe no one had said anything earlier. I couldn't believe I hadn't realized it was me! Sometimes we can miss the most obvious thing when we have too much going on.

I had a laugh, told the story to the group, turned it into a lesson on navigating stressful moments, and quickly moved on. The old me would have been rattled. I'd have put on a good face but felt stressed out and distracted. But I was able to let it go instantly in that moment.

I could have worried about what people thought of me. I could have been angry with my kids for messing around with my account. I could have been embarrassed about being so "unprofessional" (although since the pandemic, people are used to such "unprofessional" moments). But it was out of my control, so I didn't waste my energy. I let it go. Taking care of myself each day was an important part of my resilience and being able to stay calm in such moments, for the most part.

What did I not do during these first few months of the pandemic? I did NOT start working evenings and weekends again to fit it all in or run myself down. I had learned this lesson and knew I'd be more present and patient with people when I took care of myself and refueled each day. I had to practice what I preach to be my best self for my family and clients and not return to my stressed out, impatient, distracted, overwhelmed self. I had to be mindful not to resent my husband when I felt I was taking on more of the load.

I remember having a passionate discussion with a former coworker (who didn't have kids). He was telling me how his workplace was so great and flexible in its pandemic response—parents were allowed to work any hours they wanted so they could be there for their kids. Meaning they still had to put in their eight hours and get everything done, but they could put in these hours at any point in the day. To me, this sounded like a recipe for people running themselves down even more. (If this was a reality for you, know that I say this with compassion and understanding). I wholeheartedly disagreed and told him that I believed it would have been more valuable for the company to say, "You have less time in your day for work right now, so it's okay to work fewer hours. Focus on what matters most with work—drop the things that matter less."

Those few months early in the pandemic were wild. Feeling guilty about using video games as a surrogate parent to get that elusive "one more thing" done. Relearning math to be able to help with schoolwork. Kids banging on the office door when meeting with clients on Zoom. All of us trying to remain focused and calm. Saying this, I feel incredibly fortunate. So many other families and people had it far worse during this time.

THE MESSY LESSON AND KEY SHIFT

Clients, colleagues, friends—we were all trying to figure out how to juggle our work, online school, and all the uncertainty in the world. We were feeling torn between wanting to excel in our work and wanting to be there for our families and do what was best for them.

It reinforced a few lessons: Each of us has a choice about how we think about and respond to a situation. And when we take time to recharge and meet our needs, we can think and respond in a better way. We're more present and patient, we think more clearly, we make better decisions, and we have more energy. We show up in our relationships in a better way, whether at home or at work.

> **When we take care of ourselves, we can show up for others in a more meaningful way.**

Especially when the pressure is on and we are managing competing demands, particularly between work and family life. The great thing is a lot of good changes came from this experience. Employers learned to be more understanding and accommodating, recognizing the need for flexible working hours and the importance of mental health. Many people realized what truly matters to them and want more for their life. The pandemic highlighted the necessity of balance and adaptability in our daily lives, lessons that continue to influence how we approach work and family responsibilities.

This experience was another reminder for me on the delicate balance of making ourselves a priority and being there for others.

YOU MATTER TOO

You may be surprised that the advice to make yourself your number one priority has never really rung true for me. If I were truly making myself number one, there are A LOT of things I wouldn't do! Such as picking up my teen from a friend's house at midnight when I'd rather be sleeping. Or rearranging my day when a family member is in town or a team member needs something unexpectedly, even though I'd rather stick to my plan.

What I don't do anymore, though, is put myself *last* and everyone else *first*. I matter too.

YOU matter too.

"Make yourself your number one priority" can sometimes sound simplistic, even misleading. If you were to take this advice literally, your life would probably look radically different, and likely not in a caring or fulfilling way.

It's about making yourself a priority AND being there for others. A dance between taking care of your needs and caring for others. Understanding that you matter too—not above everything else, but alongside it. But make no mistake—caring for yourself is JUST as important as caring for others, and sometimes even more so.

This perspective invites you to reassess your choices and actions, ensuring they align with your personal needs, values, connections, and commitments to others. It can help you recognize that, while you might not be the only priority, you are a significant one. This is crucial to the balance—and harmony—of your life.

Now, if your tank is on empty, taking care of yourself first is the best thing to do—the idea of putting on your own oxygen mask before assisting others on the plane. When you are exhausted or burned out, it's much harder to be there for others in a meaningful way. This is not selfish. In fact, it is essential if you are going to be there for others in the best way you can. Besides, sometimes we have to be selfish!

The point is that it's not one or the other—it's about finding a balance.

A guiding question for me since my mom died as I've been learning to make my needs more of a priority is this: *Am I doing this because I care about you or I want to do it? Or am I doing this out of obligation or because I'm worried you'll be mad at me if I don't?* This helps me figure out what to say yes or no to and protect my peace, and it can help you do the same.

You can't be there for everyone. So let go of the guilt. Figure out your own balance when it comes to making yourself a priority and being there for others.

YOUR RELATIONSHIPS MATTER

It's well-known that our relationships are a biological need and one of the most important factors in our well-being and happiness. Neglecting our roles is also one of the factors that can leave us feeling seriously out of balance. We might not realize just how interconnected our work and personal lives are. When we are happier and thriving in our personal relationships, it can bring out our best selves at work (and vice versa).

How does what you've learned so far help you be a stronger leader? How does this help you be a more patient parent at the end of a long workday? How does this help you be more present and connected with your partner? You can strengthen your relationships by being more present, connecting in authentic ways, and responding in a better way when you feel frustrated. Having strong relationships with the people you care about and showing up in a way aligned with your values and who you want to be will help you be and feel more balanced. Yet, when things get too busy or difficult situations arise, we often forget that nurturing our important relationships (not ignoring or hurting them) is so important—no matter what's going on.

Whether it is your family or a team member or a friend, each positive interaction you have with another human being during your day helps both your well-being and theirs. It will lower stress levels all around.

Have compassion (and patience) when others are struggling

When it seems as if someone isn't their best self, they're likely struggling. You might feel as though you're doing all the right things but it's making no difference—the person is still having a hard time and you don't know what to do. Or perhaps you have a team member who's difficult to work with. You feel as if you're having the same conversations over and over but things aren't getting any better.

The truth is that people are usually struggling more than they let on. (Do you let other people in on how you're really doing?) They too might constantly feel as if they're not doing enough while also doing too much. Maybe they want to take something off their plate or tell you what they need but don't want to let you down.

A lot of people are in "suck it up and just get by" mode or taking their struggles out on others—remember, impatience is often a cue that someone is out of balance. In reality, they might be feeling exhausted, frustrated, disengaged and anxious. They might not be taking care of their mental health or themselves. This isn't a pass for poor behaviour. But if you keep this in mind, you'll see more room for compassion.

That said, it does take more mental energy and presence to support people who are feeling this way, especially if you're feeling this way too.

HOW DO YOU CARE FOR PEOPLE WHILE TAKING CARE OF YOU?

If you're feeling spread thin managing your own life, you might feel as if you don't have the bandwidth for other people's stuff, but even just a little caring and compassion can go a long way. It's often the small things that make the biggest difference for others.

Wondering where to find the time and energy to be there for others? First, get clear about which people are a priority in your life and need more of your time and attention. This might be your partner and kids, your team, or your closest friends. This also means getting clear on who isn't as important to you right now and who drains your energy. Doing this doesn't mean you're not a caring person—it just means you have only so much time and energy and that you're prioritizing and making intentional choices about how you spend them.

Second, understand that all that energy that goes into feeling overwhelmed or worried or frustrated could be directed to showing compassion or appreciation or kindness toward someone. It can take as little as a minute to do something caring and kind. Here are few ideas:

- Pay attention to your tone and intention in a conversation. People can tell the difference between a frustrated and a caring approach, even if the message is the same. A smile can go a long way.

- Send a quick text message or call to let someone know that you're thinking of them.
- Email someone with a specific thank-you for something they did. Acknowledge what people are doing and that they matter.
- Celebrate and acknowledge the small accomplishments each day. At team meetings, do a round table on the wins and what's good before jumping into the issues.
- Perform a random act of kindness. Buy a stranger in line a drink at a coffee shop or send flowers to someone to let them know you appreciate them.
- Be fully present—this is often the kindest thing you can do. The best gift you can give another person is your presence.

Another powerful thing you can do is check in with someone. A lot of people are overworked, overwhelmed and having a hard time. Ask them, "How are you really doing? How can I help?" Sharing your own struggles can create a safe environment for others to do the same. Make it safe for people to share then ask them what will help them (don't try to guess).

Don't underestimate the power of small caring gestures. They won't just boost others' well-being but yours as well.

And always keep in mind that it's hard to be your best when you're exhausted and spread thin. Keep giving yourself permission to take care of yourself.

BRING OUT THE BEST IN OTHERS

We want to be the best leaders, parents, friends, and people we can be. And we want the people we care about to be their happiest and best selves. While others' happiness and actions are ultimately outside of our control, we can have a positive influence. In addition to performing small acts of caring and kindness, there are many simple things you can do to set a positive tone, strengthen your relationships, and bring out the best in others.

Give people the benefit of the doubt. Most people aren't trying to be difficult. Again, if someone isn't putting their best self forward, they're likely struggling. When you give people the benefit of the doubt when they're not showing up well, you'll likely be more open in conversations with them. You'll be kinder and more patient. You'll put your attention on making the situation better. And you'll be less likely to involve your own stress and drama. This doesn't mean a free pass for people treating you poorly; however, giving the benefit of the doubt can help you to be more patient and understanding.

Support others' boundaries and needs. This is a big one in companies today with all the debates about hybrid work environments. Some employees want to return to the office, some don't. Some need flexible hours, some don't. Some want to work from the lake, some don't. Some want to be in morning meetings, some want them in the afternoons. Some might want to take an afternoon off on a nice day and catch up in the evening.

Wherever possible and healthy, be open to letting people make choices that feel good for them right now. This goes for everyone in your life.

Set a positive and optimistic tone. A positive perspective can be a buffer during periods of stress and anxiety. People tend to shy away from optimism because they feel it doesn't allow them to acknowledge when things aren't good. Again, it's not about ignoring that things are hard. It's about approaching the situation with this mindset: "Things might not be good right now. How can we make the best of it and move forward?" Positive and optimistic people are the ones who lead others through the harder times, so pay attention to the tone you set.

Focus on others' strengths. Taking the time to notice what's good about others helps you build stronger relationships with them. Recognizing and appreciating strengths also reinforces positive behaviours and attitudes. When people feel valued for what they're doing, they're more likely to continue those behaviours and feel more engaged and motivated.

Enjoy the everyday moments with others. It's okay to take a breather or be silly or enjoy the moment. Presenting in a meeting or helping your kids do their homework doesn't need to be so serious. Life doesn't need to be so serious. Give yourself and others permission to experience more joy and simplicity and fun.

Positively influence others. Influence is the ability to shape others' beliefs and behaviours, and is one of the best skills you can learn. Part of influence is getting better at making requests or asking for help, so you can get the outcome you desire or at least influence things in the direction you'd like them to go. Relationships are like bank accounts—the more we deposit in our accounts, the more we have to withdraw. When you see your deposits into your relationships as long-term investments, you'll strengthen them and also find it's much easier to influence when you need.

Being able to set a positive tone, strengthen your relationships, have more positive influence, and bring out the best in others in caring and kind ways will help you to be and feel more balanced in your life. Again, it's about balancing making yourself a priority *and* being there for others. Understanding that you matter too.

WALK YOUR TALK

Are you walking your talk? What this means is to be in integrity with your values, what you say, and model the behaviors you want to see in others. It's about giving what you want to get.

- You don't want your team working themselves into the ground? Don't do it yourself.
- You want people to remain optimistic? You remain optimistic.
- You want your team to share how they are struggling? You share.
- You want your team to take care of themselves? You take care of yourself.
- You want people to be patient and understanding? You be patient and understanding.
- You want people to listen to you? You listen to them.
- You want people to show caring and compassion? You show caring and compassion.
- You want your kids to stop yelling? You stop yelling.
- You want people to put their phones down and be present? You know what to do!

It always goes both ways, whether it's with your team, your family or anyone around you. Show how you make yourself and your personal time a priority too. Show how you manage your own well-being while balancing the demands of life and stay calm even in tough situations. Show how you interact calmly and kindly with others, even if they are being mean. Your kids and your team learn from watching you.

Walking my talk is a huge reason I have been able to remain balanced these past few years, even when life is feeling chaotic or messy. When you walk your talk, you model the behaviors you want to see. It will not only make you more effective as a leader, but more importantly, it will help you to stay in integrity with your values and the person you want to be. This isn't about perfection. We ALL have days where we don't show up as our best or do what we say. Be kind to yourself, let it go, and get back to walking your talk.

Think about how you want people to feel when they're interacting with you. How do you want your family to feel when you walk through the door? How do you want your team to see you as a leader? How can you take care of yourself and be there for others? To be present in your life and with others, and intentional to strengthen your relationships and connection?

Self-Awareness and Action:
HOW CAN YOU STRENGTHEN YOUR RELATIONSHIPS?

Reflect on these questions and write out freely whatever comes up for you without judging yourself or overthinking.

- How would you describe the strength of your relationships?

- What are the important relationships at work and in your personal life? Who is the one person you can count on the most when times get tough?

- How do you want to show up in your relationships? How do you want people to feel when they're with you?

- What actions can you take to help bring out the best in others? In what small ways can you connect with others and show you care?

- What do you need to be mindful of to better balance taking care of yourself and being there for others? How will others benefit if you make yourself a priority?

- How can you walk your talk and lead by example when it comes to being more balanced in your life?

Be bold. What is one thing you can do today to make someone else's day a little brighter and build connection? Do this.

You have everything you need to create the balance you want in your life. In the final chapter, we'll explore what it takes to keep up the momentum and see your own big shift through.

Chapter 14

LIVING YOUR BALANCED AND BOLD LIFE

"Don't get so busy making a living that you forget to make a life."

– Dolly Parton

It's been almost ten years since I started on this journey of living my balanced and bold life. Every single day (yes, every day), I'm grateful for and appreciate my life as it is while I strive for more. More joy. More impact. And more space. I'm clear on the game I'm playing.

I continue to challenge myself to grow my business within my boundaries. This means hiring people instead of doing it all myself. To do more virtual work rather than travelling while my kids are still in school. To be okay with running my business in a way that's different from others, ensuring I protect my personal time.

I want to enjoy life even more with new experiences and lake fun, while also being intentional to find the joy in the small moments each day. To be present in my life and with the people I am with and care about. I prioritize my relationship with my husband and kids above all else because, for me, the rest of it doesn't matter without them. As our two boys are now teens, I am even more aware how time is moving by.

I continue to look for ways to add more space into my calendar. I say no *all* the time so that I can say yes to what matters more. I work on stressing less in the situations that tip me off-center and grant myself grace when I let the overwhelm bubble over. I'd much rather stay home for a quiet evening than go out and I'm okay with doing life at a pace that's right for me.

I am also very aware each day of how the old, burned-out Stacey would have handled situations I face today, and I'm so thankful for all my messy lessons along the way. I know that the decision to go be with my mom that Monday morning would have been different with the old way I was operating—not because I didn't care, but because I didn't slow down enough to notice those choices and be present for the moments that matter, both big and small.

This journey has all been so worth it, and I am so much more present, calm, and happy with how I show up in my life, with myself and my important relationships.

This doesn't mean it's perfect though.

A few friends and clients have commented recently on how glamorous it must be to write a book and do more speaking. To me, it doesn't feel glamorous. It feels like I am figuring out life like everyone else—I am just far more self-aware and intentional than I used to be. While I am great at boundaries and saying no, I still worry about what people think or how my kids are doing and turn down the volume daily. I make mistakes and things don't go the way I want, but I just stress about it way less. It still amazes me how quickly our house can get messy, we're often figuring out what's for supper an hour before suppertime, and we have more debt than I'd like. I still think I will get more done in a day than I actually do.

I also know that I show up for what matters to me.

While I am ambitious and have big goals for my life, I tend to focus more on the small goals—to go for a walk, connect with my kids in the few minutes we have as we drive to school, check in with a client, put my phone away when with another person, or take the next action on a priority project, like writing this book. It has been a truly humbling experience—and probably the biggest project I've taken on since my corporate days!

While I stuck to my boundaries for the most part, I've also had to adjust them at times and be more flexible when I worked so I could write when the words flowed better. There were a couple of times before a big deadline where I ended up working most of the weekend leading up to it. While I could have moved the deadline out, I chose to continue on. It was temporary and always coming from a place of *I have a choice*, rather than *I have to do this.*

Writing this book has reminded me of just how far I've come from the days of overworking and burning out, and how I still apply so much of what I've learned to stay balanced. It also reminds me of all of my coaching clients over the years whose insights and transformations are subtly woven throughout the pages. While I didn't tell their stories, their struggles, questions, insights, actions, and experiences have been integral in shaping the guidance offered in the book. It wouldn't have happened without them and their boldness.

Overall, success to me is to be present in my life and show up for the people and things that really matter to me, and to appreciate the small moments so much more. I check in with myself each day to make sure my choices are aligning with my values and that I'm living my life rather than going through the motions.

Without my messy lessons and willingness to think about and do things differently, there's no way I'd be where I am today. I'm also a work in progress. We all are!

PAY ATTENTION TO YOUR OWN MESSY LESSONS

My wisdom was hard-won. But yours doesn't necessarily have to be. You can use everything I've shared with you in this book to create your own balanced life, in a way that works for you. You're absolutely capable.

At the same time, I invite you to pay attention to your own messy lessons. When we make mistakes or don't meet our own expectations, we have a chance to learn and change our ways. To make new choices. Our most important lessons usually arise from our struggles and when we step out of what's comfortable for us. Don't just accept things as they are, but be bold enough to ask how you can make them better, while taking the pressure off and being kind to yourself as you grow. This helps not just you, but also your relationships, your work, and how you lead by example.

Remember, when you're living out of whack with your values, lack boundaries, or have a hard time saying no, you'll experience more stress, undercut your performance, and struggle unnecessarily. But, like a rock being dropped in the water, when you start to make some positive changes, you'll send out positive ripples in every direction. Your work will benefit, your relationships will benefit, and you will benefit.

You can resign yourself to "just getting by" and wait for the day when things will be "better," or you start to make the best of it now and begin living in a way that aligns with what truly matters to you. You can start to work less, live more, and be your best at work and at home. You can think and do something different. You can find a pace that's right for you. You can decide not to settle for the status quo.

You can make your own big shift in how you're showing up in your life.

And you can do this now. Not in five years, or one year, or six months, but right now. No matter your age or your circumstances or your position. No matter how burned out or busy you might be.

This comes with being intentional.

SHOW UP WITH INTENTION EVERY DAY

Living a balanced life takes intention. It takes being mindful of your choices, the person you're being, and how you're showing up in your life. It takes being clear on your values, boundaries, and real priorities. It also takes saying no a whole lot more. To no longer settle for feeling exhausted and overwhelmed each day.

As you implement what you've discovered about yourself in this book, here are a few key perspectives to keep in mind when it comes to living YOUR balanced and bold life.

Appreciate the small, ordinary moments. I used to think it was the career, the house, and the vacations that made life bigger and better. And these things do offer experiences, joy, and meaning. But what I've learned over the years is that getting the small, everyday moments right (being present and showing up in the way you want) is what truly makes life bigger and better. These little things add up to big things. Maybe when your kid comes into the room to tell you something that happened in their day, you stop everything to be fully present with them. Or when a team member comes to you with a concern, you take the time to genuinely listen and help. Maybe when you're feeling tired or overwhelmed, you rest or ask for help or say no to something. Maybe when you're out walking your dog, you appreciate the beauty of nature or you look at the person you're talking to (not at your phone).

When you slow down the pace, you can be more present in the day-to-day moments that offer joy and peace. These moments can feel like time-outs from daily busyness. When you're present in them, a sense of stillness arises and the concerns and stressors of the day seem to evaporate.

An extraordinary life can come from getting the ordinary moments right.

Give yourself permission to focus on what really matters. Over and over. It's okay to stop trying to do it all. Everything you discovered about yourself you'll revisit again and again. Your values, boundaries, and priorities will evolve over time.

The more I have on the go, the more intentional I am about ensuring I have space for my priorities, saying no to what I no longer have room for, and refueling my tank daily and as I need.

Embrace the "And". As we make our way through life, we often face situations that seem to demand that a choice be made between two seemingly conflicting perspectives or actions. *And* allows space for both. It creates a sense of harmony and flexibility. This helps us recognize the complexity of our emotions and experiences, allowing us to approach challenges with a more well-rounded perspective. It offers us more of a balance—not that it must be equal—but to create room and space to flex along a continuum. Such as . . .

- Needing alone time *and* enjoying being with other people
- Wanting structure *and* flexibility in your calendar
- Caring about someone *and* not wanting to be around them
- Focusing on a plan *and* being open to unexpected opportunities
- Having a daily routine *and* leaving room for spontaneity
- Holding strong opinions *and* being open to different perspectives
- Excelling in your work *and* personal life

- Feeling happy in life *and* overwhelmed some days
- Feeling grateful for everything you have now *and* aspiring to more
- Being your best self *and* a work in progress.

The list could go on and on. The power of *and* is simple yet profound. It can take the pressure off. It can help you to experience more ease and less conflict. It can help you to create your own sense of balance.

Remember to be present, not perfect. This is so important. The present moment is where we truly live. Remembering that your life is happening now can help you be more present. Let go of having to be the perfect leader or perfect mom—seriously, we all mess up. It's your presence with the people you care about that truly matters. There are only so many evenings left until your kids go to college, only so many days you'll be able to spend at the lake. You don't get this time back. Allow your awareness of transience—of how finite time is—to keep guiding you back to what's most important. Seize the small moments before they exit, unannounced and unappreciated. Being more present in your life, physically and mentally, will help you to feel far more balanced. Build your mindfulness muscle and keep practicing being present. It does get easier, I promise.

Celebrate and acknowledge the wins—every single day. In the relentless pursuit of success and being hard on ourselves, it's easy to overlook the small victories. Yet focusing on these wins, no matter how minor they might seem, is crucial for your happiness, confidence, and performance. Doing so leads to a positive mindset. Especially if you always feel as if you're not doing enough.

As you wrap up your day, rather than dwelling on tasks left undone or goals yet to be reached, take a few moments to reflect on and celebrate what you did accomplish and how you did show up or the lesson you learned. This practice isn't just about giving yourself a pat on the back; it's a powerful tool for reinforcing positive behaviours and building confidence. Whether you've successfully navigated a challenging meeting, made a little progress on a long-term project, or simply managed your time effectively, acknowledging these things can provide a sense of fulfillment and perspective.

Know that your best will look different on different days. This is a lesson I've learned over and over! I have high expectations of myself and strive for excellence in my work, as a parent, for myself, and more. And sometimes, when I find myself not as productive as I *think* I should be, I fall into an old habit of being hard on myself. I'll tell myself that I'm procrastinating or not living up to my best . . . when what I really need is to take a step back and reset. Which is completely okay. We aren't meant to be one-hundred-percent consistent all the time. Again, be kind to yourself.

You'll have days where you struggle. You'll have days where unexpected things happen and you need to adjust. You'll have days where you're less focused or not showing up as the leader or parent or high performer you want to be. You'll have days where you knock it out of the park in one area and fall short of your expectations in another.

Keep in mind that being kind to yourself doesn't mean settling for the way things are. If you're unhappy about something in your life, you can change it. Just remember that your best will look different on different days. Cut yourself some slack.

Work with your desired end in mind. Imagine yourself six months in the future. You're making the most out of your days and living in a way that makes you proud and more balanced in your life. Who are you being? What are you thinking about and doing differently? How are you showing up in your life? How do you feel? Vividly imagine yourself in that ideal life as your ideal self. Be as specific as you can.

Now, what would your future self tell you to do now? What would you go for if you weren't worried about what people might think? Let this guide your choices.

Be bold. Inside all of us, I believe there is the part that has the courage to make the leap for what we really want and the life we want to live. And inside all of us is the part that wants to play it safe, keep everyone else happy and not rock the boat. This can be speaking up in a meeting or saying no to someone—or the bigger life decisions to go for what you truly want. Let your bold side out. Your future self will thank you for it.

WHAT'S YOUR GUIDEPOST?

You must truly *want* to live a balanced life in order to have one. When life is feeling chaotic, what will give you the inner motivation to live in a way that's aligned with your values? What will help you to stay focused on the right things and not get pulled into everyone else's demands and expectations? What's a question or perspective that will center you?

> **Think of your guidepost as your North Star—something consistent you can return to if you're feeling lost.**

A guidepost is a deeply ingrained principle or value that keeps us anchored to what truly matters. It's a reference point that helps us navigate life's messy choices and challenges, ensuring we remain true to ourselves. In moments of doubt or confusion, our guidepost offers clarity, reminding us of what our hearts are truly aligned with.

My guidepost is: *What if this were my last day alive?*

Yes, a little morbid, I know. But this helps me stay present and live in a way I want. To find the joy every single day. Not wishing or waiting for something to happen. Not stewing about something that happened in the past. Not getting so caught up in goals that I forget to appreciate what I have now. I want to connect deeply with the people around me in the everyday moments.

As I mentioned at the start of the book, I don't want to be the person who needs something bad to happen to slow down, be more present, and be the person I want to be. So every time I'm feeling frustrated about something I can't seem to shake, I ask myself that question to guide me: *What if this were my last day alive?* Or, *What if someone I love deeply is gone tomorrow*? It instantly centers me. Whatever I am in a tizzy about goes away. It keeps me grateful for everything I have and to keep taking action toward what I want for my life.

What's your guidepost?

LIVING YOUR BALANCED AND BOLD LIFE
You now have a path forward by . . .

Remembering that your life is happening now
Being self-aware and real with yourself
Owning your mindset, time, and what's possible
Living and leading with your values

Protecting your time and energy with boundaries
Being clear on your real priorities and what matters less
Saying no so you can say yes to what matters more
Being present, not perfect
Stepping out of the overwhelm
Turning down the volume on worry and guilt
Feeling more confident in yourself and your choices
Doing more of what gives you joy and less of what stresses you out
Navigating the tougher times with more ease and resilience
Making yourself a priority *and* being there for others

These areas will look different in your life than they do in mine. We all have our own values, boundaries, and priorities. We all have various things that help us to feel and be our best. We each have our own version of balance and success.

You won't make all the changes at once, and small actions can make a big difference. The goal isn't to be perfect or to make every area of your life equal, but to create more harmony overall. To have more time and energy for what really matters. To work less but contribute in a deeper way. To make your happiness and well-being a priority and take care of yourself so that you can navigate the tougher times with more ease and be there for others in a more meaningful way. To be more present in your life. To be your best self at work and home, even with all the demands and messiness of everyday life. And to grant yourself grace when you don't.

Remember, you don't find balance—you create it.

MY NOTE TO YOU

If there's still a teeny tiny part of you wondering if you're actually going to do something different, consider this note.

Dear _____,

Slow down for a moment.
Take a deep breath.
Know that you're capable and more than good enough.
It's amazing how you've been handling it all.
But something has to give.
You have too much on your plate.
The answer isn't working harder.
You must say no to what matters less.
You must say yes to what matters more.
There is a better way.
You will feel like yourself again.
You will lead even stronger.
You will enjoy your days far more.
See, this is urgent and important.
It's your life we're talking about.
No one is coming to save you.
It starts with you.
And right now, something has to change.
Be bold.
Don't settle for the way things are.
You've got this.

Love, Stacey

This is what I would have told myself all those years ago when I started on this journey. This is what I want to say to you now. Trust that the path is there for you to be happier, balanced, and successful. You just have to give yourself permission to take it.

Self-Awareness and Action:
WHAT'S YOUR NEXT MOVE?

Reflect on these questions and write out freely whatever comes up for you without judging yourself or overthinking.

- What were your biggest insights and takeaways about yourself after reading this book? What was the MOST valuable to you? These stood out to you for a reason, so pay attention!

- What does your ideal future and self look like? What would your future self come back to tell you to do now?

- Why is it important to you to make the changes you want to make in your life? Who else will benefit?

- What small daily actions will help you show up with intention and stay aligned with what you want?

- What's your guidepost? What will help you follow through in creating the balance you want in your life?

Be bold. What are you no longer willing to settle for? Commit to doing something right now—today—to create your balanced and bold life.

Because your life is happening right now.
And you don't want to miss it!

A Final Nudge

BE THE POSITIVE RIPPLE

"The people who are crazy enough to think they can change the world are the ones who do."

– Rob Siltanen

Early on in my business, my intuition led me to a deep desire to help others be more balanced in their lives, both as leaders and for themselves. In January 2017, I wrote my first blog post, "What Does Work-Life Balance Even Mean?", which started me on this writing path. Over the years, I've taken on other focus areas, such as resilience, leadership, and communication, and I've found that balance has been a core theme in all of them. A calling within me, you could say.

More people than I can count have also told me that it's a waste of effort to focus on balance, saying things such as, "You'll never change the corporate rat race", "Balance is impossible", "People don't really want that", "Focus on improving at work or at home, but not both—it's too big an ambition", "Call it something else", and, as I shared earlier, "You can't be happy, balanced, and successful. You get two out of the three if you're lucky." Thankfully, I didn't let other people's voices drown out my intuition.

I believe that you and others do want more balance. You want to enjoy your life and do well in your work. To be more present and calmer with your family. To take care of yourself and feel happier. To work less and live more. To be your best self, both at work and at home. So that the people you care about the most get the best of you, not just what's left of you. This is what I wanted all those years ago when I made my first bold decision to stop working so much. And it's what I want today.

Each day, this inner nudge inspires me to keep writing and teaching and coaching others in this space and let go of my doubts and worries about what people might think. I've had to walk my talk and find the courage to share my stories and what I've learned in the hopes it will help you in your own way—and so that you can be the positive ripple for others.

One day early in 2023, about a year before I wrote this page for you, my doubts about making balance the main focus of my business were high. I found myself letting other people's opinions and skepticism creep in, and I wondered if I was really meant to be doing this and if I could effect real and meaningful change at the level to which I aspired.

I'd been working on a new vision board for a few weeks and had purchased about 140 used *Oprah* magazines from a garage sale so I could cut out words and pictures that aligned with my aspirations and goals. On this day, feeling deflated in my work, I decided to finish up the vision board, wanting to do something creative. I'd already gone through about forty magazines in the past few weeks, and I told myself I was going to go through only one or two more on that day and be done.

Instead of just picking the next one off the pile, I let my intuition choose. I closed my eyes, ran my fingers along all the magazines, and then selected one that seemed to nudge me. It was an issue from 2003—and it was all about balance. I took that as a sign.

But the next thing that happened was the *real sign.*

While flipping through the magazine, I got to the main article on balance, by Martha Beck. Across the two-page spread was an image of an elephant balanced on a beach ball—*the exact same photo I'd used in my first blog post!* Tearing up, I found my inner confidence. I knew without a doubt that this was, in fact, what I was meant to do and how I could help others. If I could make even one person's life better, it would be worth it—though the goal is to impact far more than one, which we can do together.

Since then, I haven't doubted my mission to help others be more balanced and present in how they live and lead, and that's what gave me the courage and commitment to finally write this book. To make a bigger positive ripple.

To inspire you to make yourself a priority, to be the leader you wish you had, to be the parent you want to be, and to lead by example and create a positive ripple effect: for your team, your family, and the people around you. We can be happier, balanced, and successful, whatever that looks like for each of us.

Always remember you have a choice. At this very moment, you can change your life. You can be intentional about being balanced in your life. Every moment offers you a choice to be the person you want to be and live the life you want to live.

And in the moments when you feel as if you're screwing it up and you're frustrated and overwhelmed, know that there's nothing wrong with you for feeling this way or wanting to slow it down and take life at a pace that's right for you. It might not feel easy to make the choices you know you need and want to make. But I can promise you that being (and feeling) balanced *is* easier than feeling overwhelmed, burned out, or exhausted every single day.

So give yourself permission to live your balanced and bold life—for yourself and others.

We are the positive ripple.

ACKNOWLEDGMENTS

First and foremost, a big thank-you to my number one fan, pep talker, and chief editor for the past eight years: my husband, Kenton. Many of the blog and social media posts you edited over the past few years ended up in this book, and you were a huge help in getting these pages to where they needed to be. Thank you for being my extra set of eyes, helping me narrow down my many ideas and cut where needed (it's so hard to cut!), and being patient with me when I wanted to get the words "just right" on paper. You are my best friend, my biggest cheerleader, and such an important part of bringing this book to life. Thank you with all my heart.

A huge thank-you to my editor, Rachel, who was the very first person to read the very first draft. You returned it to me with such encouragement and vital changes. Your willingness to collaborate to ensure it felt like my voice, make the book so much better, and bring genuine excitement to this project has been invaluable. To my book designer, Vanessa, who professionally and strikingly brought my vision to life on the cover and added some colour to it, and to Carla, who captured the perfect photo for it. Thank you. I wanted a professional cover that offered a smile and the vibe of *come on this journey with me*, and you helped me create that vision. (The full names of these professionals are on the copyright page).

Thank you to the wonderful women, many of whom are clients turned friends, who read the book in advance and provided instrumental feedback—both the positive feedback—which helped give me the courage to see things through—and the important, specific feedback, which made the book so much better for the reader. Your insights helped tremendously. A special thanks to Tanya, Julie, Catherine, Lisa, Allison, Amie, and Joanna, and to Meghan, who not only offered feedback but also shared her story in the opening chapter. I so appreciate your time, as well as your willingness to overlook the typos and read an unfinished version! You are all gems.

I must also acknowledge and thank all my clients, former colleagues, and others I've worked with over the years whose insights and transformations are woven throughout these pages. Your struggles, questions, aha moments, actions, and experiences were essential in helping to shape the guidance offered in the book. Thank you for your boldness and for showing up for yourself. This book wouldn't have happened without you.

Thank you to everyone else who helped bring this book into the world, including mentors, authors whose works inspired and encouraged me, those who helped with small (yet essential) parts of the book publishing process, and so many others along the way.

Thank you to friends and family in my small inner circle. Your ongoing encouragement and support have meant so much. Thank you to my kids. You keep me present, grounded, and intentional to be the parent and person I want to be.

Lastly, thank you to YOU, the reader. By choosing yourself and for being the positive ripple. By living these principles and even sharing the book with others, you help extend the reach and impact of the ideas. The true influence of a book is realized through its readers who embrace and share its message.

If I missed anyone, I'll include you the next go-around. I appreciate you all!

REFERENCES

Gretchen Rubin, "What You Do Every Day Matters More Than What You Do Once In a While," *The Happiness Project* (blog), November 7, 2011, https://gretchenrubin.com/articles/what-you-do-every-day-matters-more-than-what-you-do-once-in-a-while

Maya Angelou (@DrMayaAngelou), "Do the best you can until you know better. Then when you know better, do better," X, August 12, 2018, https://twitter.com/DrMayaAngelou/status/1028663286512930817?lang=en

Jen Fisher, "Lessons from a Groundbreaking New Report on Well-Being," Thrive Global, https://community.thriveglobal.com/lessons-from-a-groundbreaking-new-report-on-well-being

Anne Lamott, "Almost everything will work again if you unplug it for a few minutes, including you," X (@TEDTalks), June 17, 2017, https://twitter.com/TEDTalks/status/876079553969627136?lang=en

Jerzy Gregorek, "Hard choices, easy life. Easy choices, hard life," in Tim Ferriss, *Tribe of Mentors: Short Life Advice from the Best in the World* (2017)

"Work-life Balance: Make it your business," Canadian Mental Health Association, September 21, 2021, https://cmha.ca/brochure/work-life-balance-make-it-your-business

Shawn Achor, *The Happiness Advantage: The Seven Principles of Positive Psychology That Fuel Success and Performance at Work* (2010)

LeanIn.Org and McKinsey & Company, *Women in the Workplace 2022*, Lean In, https://leanin.org/women-in-the-workplace/2022

LeanIn.Org and McKinsey & Company, *Women in the Workplace 2023*, Lean In, https://www.mckinsey.com/featured-insights/diversity-and-inclusion/women-in-the-workplace

"A shorter working week for everyone: How much paid work is needed for mental health and well-being?" *Social Science & Medicine* 241 (November 2019), https://doi.org/10.1016/j.socscimed.2019.06.006

"Researchers have found that we're 31% more productive when our brains are in a positive state": from Achor, *The Happiness Advantage* (2010)

A study conducted by John Pencavel of Stanford University explored the relationship between working hours and productivity: "The Productivity of Working Hours," *Economic Journal* 125, no. 589 (December 2015), https://doi.org/10.1111/ecoj.12166

"Arianna Huffington On What She Wishes She Knew When She Was 20" *Time Magazine* (June 2016), https://time.com/4347144/arianna-huffington-twenty/

A significant trial of the four-day workweek was conducted in the UK from June to December 2022. https://www.businessinsider.com/most-companies-biggest-4-day-work-week-trial-made-permanent-2024

"The happiest people don't have the best of everything—they just make the best of everything they have" comes from an unknown author.

Marshall Goldsmith. *What Got You Here Won't Get You There: How Successful People Become Even More Successful* (2007)

Hugo Alberts, Mindfulness X program, PositivePsychology.com, 2024, accessed 2019. https://pro.positivepsychology.com/product/mindfulness-x-complete-8-week-mindfulness-training/

Brené Brown, *Daring Greatly: How the Courage to Be Vulnerable Transforms the Way We Live, Love, Parent, and Lead* (2012)

Cyril Northcote Parkinson, *Parkinson's Law: The Pursuit of Progress* (1957)

Greg McKeown, *Essentialism: The Disciplined Pursuit of Less* (2014)

Gary Keller and Jay Papasan, *The ONE Thing: The Surprisingly Simple Truth About Extraordinary Results* (2013)

REFERENCES

Michael Bungay Stanier, "We love saying yes. We find it hard to say no. And it turns out saying a clear and kind No is one of the secrets to a better life." LinkedIn, 2023. URL unavailable.

Michael Bungay Stanier, *The Coaching Habit: Say Less, Ask More & Change the Way You Lead Forever* (2016)

Adam Grant (@AdamMGrant), "Balance rarely comes from increasing efficiency. It usually involves reducing responsibilities. The more priorities we have, the harder they are to juggle. It's better to do a few things well than be overwhelmed by many. A key to avoiding burnout is deciding what doesn't matter," X, April 1, 2023, https://twitter.com/AdamMGrant/status/1642180266234990594

Deepak Chopra, "Top 30 Deepak Chopra Quotes," Chopra, August 28, 2018, https://chopra.com/blogs/personal-growth/top-30-deepak-chopra-quotes

Alan Watts, *The Wisdom of Insecurity: A Message for an Age of Anxiety* (2011)

Hugo Alberts, Mindfulness X program, PositivePsychology.com, 2024, accessed 2019. https://pro.positivepsychology.com/product/mindfulness-x-complete-8-week-mindfulness-training/

Shawn Achor, *The Happiness Advantage: The Seven Principles of Positive Psychology That Fuel Success and Performance at Work* (2010)

Tal Ben-Shahar, *Choose the Life You Want: The Mindful Way to Happiness* (2014)

Bronnie Ware, *The Top Five Regrets of the Dying: A Life Transformed by the Dearly Departing* (2019)

Sharon Salzberg, *Real Happiness: The Power of Meditation: A 28-Day Program* (2010)

Jen Sincero, *You Are a Badass®: How to Stop Doubting Your Greatness and Start Living an Awesome Life* (2013)

Tim Ferriss, *The 4-Hour Workweek: Escape the 9–5, Live Anywhere, and Join the New Rich* (2009)

Eleanor Roosevelt quote attributed to various sources. Exact original source not verified.

Positive Psychology: Resilience Skills, University of Pennsylvania, Coursera, 2017. https://www.coursera.org/learn/positive-psychology-resilience

Maya Angelou, "Maya Angelou in Her Own Words," *Success* (blog), *Success Magazine*, September 19, 2011, https://www.success.com/maya-angelou-in-her-own-words

Confidence definition aligns with Oxford English Dictionary, Oxford Languages

Brendon Burchard, "And then one day I decided that hurry and stress were no longer going to be part of my life" Meta, March 14, 2015, https://www.facebook.com/photo?fbid=931003446933283&set=and-then-one-day-i-decided-that-hurry-and-stress-were-no-longer-going-to-be-part

Steve Maraboli, *Life, the Truth, and Being Free* (2009)

L.R. Knost (@lrknost), "Taking care of myself doesn't mean 'me first.' It means 'me, too,'" Instagram, December 5, 2019, https://www.instagram.com/lrknost/p/B5sguJ0HkuB

Dolly Parton (@DollyParton), "Don't get so busy making a living that you forget to make a life," X, August 9, 2010, 12:21 p.m., https://twitter.com/DollyParton/status/20723962228?lang=en

Rob Siltanen, "The Real Story Behind Apple's 'Think Different' Campaign," Forbes, December 14, 2011. https://www.forbes.com/sites/onmarketing/2011/12/14/the-real-story-behind-apples-think-different-campaign/

O, The Oprah Magazine, Volume 4, Number 4, April 2003. Martha Beck, "Balance" *O, The Oprah Magazine*, April 2003.

Elephant photo by Bob Elsdale.

ABOUT THE AUTHOR

STACEY OLSON, CPPC, works with leaders and teams who want to create more balance, stress less, and perform even better. She is a Leadership and Positive Psychology Certified Coach, has more than fifteen years of corporate and business experience, and has gone through her own transformational change from being close to burnout to figuring out how to be more balanced, feel happier, and accomplish even more. She helps others through coaching, workshops, and speaking—and now this book! Stacey lives in Canada with her husband and kids, loves spending time at the lake, and is on a mission to empower more balance and presence in our everyday lives and leadership.

Connect with and follow Stacey on LinkedIn at www.linkedin.com/in/stacey-olson-cppc

You can also access on-demand
courses and programs on her website, including:

The Confident "No" Masterclass

*The Big Shift: Focus Your Time,
Balance Your Life Workshop Series*

The Balanced Leader™ Program

To learn more and to book Stacey to speak virtually or in person at your event, visit: **www.staceyolson.ca**

To access free resources that support this book,
go to **www.staceyolson.ca/balance**

Thank you for reading *Your Balanced and Bold Life: Work Less, Live More, and Be Your Best!*

Please share your key insights, a photo of you with the book, and/or feedback on social media using these hashtags and handles:

**#balancedleaders and #yourbalancedandboldlife
@staceyolsonaim**

Consider recommending this book to someone you think would benefit from it. Let's be the positive ripple together!

And finally, if you enjoyed this book, I'd be so grateful if you could leave a review on Amazon, Goodreads, or wherever you like to review books. Your support is incredibly valuable in helping others find this book and spread the message.

P.S. I'm here cheering you on.
You've got this!

www.ingramcontent.com/pod-product-compliance
Lightning Source LLC
Chambersburg PA
CBHW030544080526
44585CB00012B/255